T0150389

SINGING IN THE DARK

PRAISE FOR THE BOOK

'The range and depth of this amazing anthology convey the conflicted and conflicting emotions of our times. It provides the consolations of poetry and the solace of art as balm to troubled souls'—Namita Gokhale, author, and director, Jaipur Literature Festival

'Perhaps no catastrophe has ever struck human life with power as pervasive as the pandemic. While the benumbed world is struggling to combat the apocalyptic devastation it has wreaked, a choral spectrum of poetry has emerged to rekindle the spirit of hope. Has poetry not always spelt hope in dark times? Over a hundred voices of unparalleled resilience have gathered here to speak in a "jumbled mix of words" to carry a "sky of memories". Sharing the "earth's breathing", they have burst forth into a "slipstream of time". In each of them, the word of the poet rises across nations reduced to the "size of a mouse hole" to envision "the anguish of mountains". It is a word of love, solace and bonding; the word the world today is sorely in need of hearing'—Gulammohammed Sheikh, artist and author

'I salute this effort and extend sincere congratulations to all the poets included in the anthology. Although it may seem that devoting poetic energy to an invisible enemy that is pushing the world towards a terrifying future is too closely tied to social duty, the truth is entirely different: it is not death that the poets are celebrating, it is life'—Evald Flisar, Slovenian author and playwright

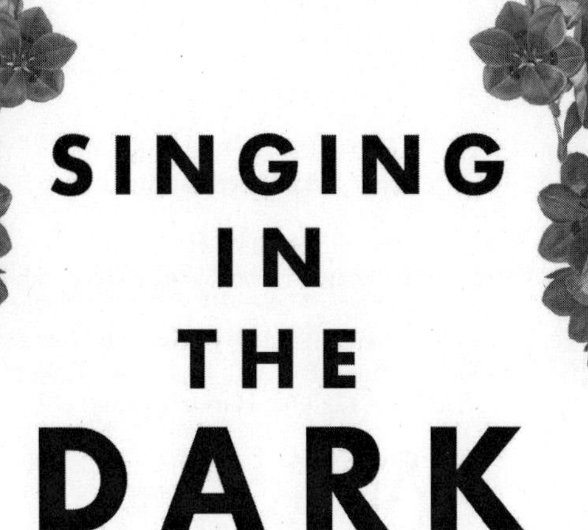

SINGING IN THE DARK

A GLOBAL ANTHOLOGY *OF* POETRY UNDER LOCKDOWN

EDITED BY

K. SATCHIDANANDAN & NISHI CHAWLA

VINTAGE

An imprint of Penguin Random House

VINTAGE

USA | Canada | UK | Ireland | Australia
New Zealand | India | South Africa | China

Vintage is part of the Penguin Random House group of companies
whose addresses can be found at global.penguinrandomhouse.com

Published by Penguin Random House India Pvt. Ltd
7th Floor, Infinity Tower C, DLF Cyber City,
Gurgaon 122 002, Haryana, India

Published in Vintage by Penguin Random House India 2020

Page 361 is an extension of the copyright page

Book design and layout by Devangana Dash

10 9 8 7 6 5 4 3 2 1

ISBN 9780670094479

Typeset in Crimson Text by Manipal Technologies Limited, Manipal
Printed at Replika Press Pvt. Ltd, India

www.penguin.co.in

In the dark times
Will there also be singing?
Yes, there will also be singing.
About the dark times.

Bertolt Brecht, 'Motto'

Rich men, trust not in wealth,
Gold cannot buy you health;
Physic himself must fade.
All things to end are made,
The plague full swift goes by;
I am sick, I must die.
Lord, have mercy on us!

Strength stoops unto the grave,
Worms feed on Hector brave;
Swords may not fight with fate,
Earth still holds open her gate.
Lord, have mercy on us!

Thomas Nashe, 'A Litany in Time of Plague'

CONTENTS

FOREWORD

At the dawn of the global pandemic early in 2020, we began thinking of bringing out an international anthology of poems that reflects the mood of these times when human beings are threatened on an unprecedented scale by a pandemic reminiscent of the destruction caused in earlier ages by plagues and other epidemics. We had in our mind James Joyce's famous saying about writers, 'Squeeze us, we are olives', and Bertolt Brecht's lines, 'Will there be singing in bad times? Yes, singing about dark times', both of which remind us of the anguish at the root of all genuine creativity.

This is indeed a time of deep reflection as the first global pandemic of the social media age. Its spread has necessarily evoked introspection, especially on the relationship of human beings and nature, among poets and artists who are the most sensitive representatives of the human species. Poets look at this altered sense of reality in their own special ways, and we asked ourselves what it means to write poetry inspired by and about the COVID-19 pandemic. We did realize that poets typically privilege a slow churning of their art, and that not many poets would embrace the idea of immediately responding to the pandemic as it is shaping and reshaping our lives. Yet, we were pleasantly surprised by the overwhelming response from a global community of established and well-respected poets. We were also pleased by the ease and facility with which we got publishing rights from so many poets with strong literary credentials, from Europe, India, Israel, Palestine, East Asia, Australia, Africa and the Americas.

We believe that all of these poets have been rendered so vulnerable, along with the rest of humanity, that they were moved to project their brutally changed reality amid the unique and poignant consequences of the pandemic. We are convinced that the personal experiences of the lockdown that have been recorded in these fine poems and their possible ramifications, biographical or autobiographical, true or fictive, real or imagined, will offer an invaluable poetic record for all future readers to experience first-hand our dramatically altered times. Some poets have experimented with the vast possibilities of technique and thought, and others have reflected in a philosophical spirit on their personal journey. The anthology will well serve the purpose of capturing the anguish and the trauma, the anger and the befuddlement, as well as the hope for returning to the certainty of the world order that the pandemic has destroyed or the movement towards a more just and egalitarian world. As poets and academics ourselves, we approach poetry with a strong commitment to the literary traditions that challenge readers and promote a strenuous engagement of the imagination. We have received a vast array of poems that provoke readers to new experiences of rendering transparent the raw opacity of our altered situation, analysing complexity, and discovering, in the concrete density of their poems, a new aesthetic and new meanings for themselves.

It is, of course, 'writing from the heart' that we have looked for. However, at the same time, the poems we have received from more than one hundred poets from twenty languages are diverse kinds of emotional and intellectual journeys that bring out in subtle ways our human dilemmas and our predicaments, our introspection and retrospection, our response to social isolation and physical distancing, and some common but significantly shared experience. We are firmly convinced that a collection of poems that addresses the existential experiences and responses of these well-recognized poets from across the globe will be remembered and cherished by generations of readers to come. We have arranged them in a simple alphabetical order so as to eliminate any kind of hierarchy. We sincerely hope these lonely voices of hope, despair and meditation will resonate with every lover of poetry.

Nishi Chawla, K. Satchidanandan

August 2020

USHA AKELLA

has authored four books of poetry, one chapbook, and scripted/produced one musical drama. She recently earned a master's in creative writing from Cambridge University, UK. Her latest poetry book, *The Waiting*, was published by the Sahitya Akademi. She is the founder of Matwaala, the first South Asian Diaspora Poetry Festival in the US (www.matwaala.com).

CAVED—7.8 BILLION

1

This one looks like a planet of red windmills whirring
or a field of poppies, a wild corona of a star, heart of sunflower,
this pretty thing is fanged, arsenal in Death's stockpile,
small unseen things are perfectly precise,
Hanuman burnt the city of Lanka thus, eroding pride.

2

The bush is bursting with red berries,
spring has slipped through the crevices breathing green on
the city,
a musician plays his oud to the sky in himself,
the trees are gravestones to the forgotten dead,
the deer conglomerate driven to community,
more families staked by windows notice the heartbeat of nature.

3

The camera has vertigo, it's a crazy arc
leering on the hoarded splendour of one family,
(what madness was this to record and proudly share?)
lines of bottles on the kitchen cabinetry
riddled with oil of bright urine hue,
toilet rolls, bounties, tissues, food cans,
a pantry full of debris for doomsday,
this raid of the innards of stores,
this back-to-basics, to Freud's Id of fear and self-first.

4

Where do we send our unclaimed sorrow?
The unlabelled debris of life?
The racking cough of unprocessed wounds?
There is no island to send them off, be done, be free.
Like those lines of caskets in dirt in Hart island,

where New York City is belching unclaimed bodies
its gut overflowing.

5
The mind is like an abacus now
computing deaths on the excel sheet
of consciousness; from the Spanish flu 20-50 million,
from the Black plague 50 million, from COVID . . .
what black hole continues to gorge up souls
or is it an empyrean of hopeful light,
what joust happens in the universe's annals
between what forces, this unending play
into and out of life, where is that mighty
being who once gave the song of life
to a tremulous warrior's heart in the middle of battle?
Each of us is a naive question as we have always been
curved like an embryo, full-stopped by death.

J. JOY MATTHEWS ALFORD

was appointed the inaugural Poet Laureate of Prince George's County, Maryland, in September 2018. Also known as 'Sistah Joy', she is an author, arts advocate, and produces and has hosted the award-winning poetry-based cable television show, *Sojourn with Words*, since its inception in 2005. Sistah Joy received the Poet Laureate Special Award (2002) in her native Washington, D.C. In 1995, she founded the socially conscious poetry ensemble, Collective Voices, which has performed nationally and internationally. Sistah Joy is the author of three books, *Lord I'm Dancin' As Fast As I Can* (2000); *From Pain to Empowerment: The Fabric of My Being* (2009); and *This Garden Called Life* (2011).

KITCHEN WINDOW

Standing here
the world looks bright.
Squirrels still scamper
and red-breasted robins hop
amid my freshly cut lawn.
A lone but lovely lilac bush
and soon to bloom forsythia
soothe my spirit.
All seems right with the world
through this window.
Countless have been the tranquil hours
we have shared. She has been my respite,
affording me moments of peace and
serenity amid life's tumultuous storms,
shielding me, albeit momentarily,
from some of life's harshest realities.
Her gently framed view of the world
provides, even now, a pastoral view
that is sacred to my soul.
I come to this sacred space
knowing it has been given to me
for times such as this
when reality overwhelms
and would deny the notion
that beauty still exists—
this space where even washing a dish
can return calm and control to my life
banishing such blight as disease and pandemics,
signals that the ravages of devastation and loss
linger so very close by.

ANVAR ALI

is a poet, documentary film-maker, lyricist and translator. His three collections of poetry established him as one of the prominent voices in contemporary Indian poetry. His poems have been translated into various Indian and foreign languages. He has won two international awards and a state award for the screenplay of *Margam*, the feature film he has co-written. *Call from the Other Shore*, a biopic on Attoor Ravi Varma, the renowned Malayalam poet, is his first independent documentary film. He participated in the Writer-in-Residence Program of Literature Translation Institute, South Korea, in 2007 and has represented Malayalam poetry at various national and international writers' meets and festivals.

THE SONG OF SONGS*

It went off startling the cities.
The scattered bones
didn't become the destination
nor the stones a punishment.

From measured distances,
each city heard its bark.
Each channel was filled with its foam.

Since there was no more distinction
between the body and the soul
it passed
formless
as incarnate speed.

*

Renuncees of the future, know
one day
this journey will end
on the tip of a rubbish heap.

The nervous system
that had been circulating
the anarchist electricity everywhere
will that day reverberate
as a single string.

It will hug and crush
and explode the last vowel.

---

* *Translated from the Malayalam by K. Satchidanandan.*

From then on
the rubbish dumps of earth
will give birth to
rivers that will drown
heaven and hell.
Love's army, all nude,
Will stand guard to it.

Nothing that is not mad
will have entry there.

SMELL*

A damn smell,
tired from wandering
through all the air and draft,
would come knocking
on the soot-covered door
one day.

Serving
the last drop of blood
from its heart,
the body
would sigh.

Then,
a suicide truck of the wind
would rush inside,
bearing the death-smell
of all that ran away.

---

* *Translated from the Malayalam by Rizio Raj.*

KUMAR AMBUJ

is the author of seven anthologies of poetry and a collection of short stories. He has also edited a number of publications, including an issue of the reputed magazine of contemporary Hindi poetry, *Vasudha*, and a book on the Gujarat riots of 2002. His poetry has been translated into several languages and has been included in several anthologies and collections. His awards include the Bharat Bhushan Agarwal Puraskar, Makhanlal Chaturvedi Puraskar, Vageeshwari Puraskar, Shrikant Verma Samman, Girija Kumar Mathur Samman and Kedar Samman, to name a few. He lives in Bhopal.

OFFICIAL DEATHS ARE A SUPERSTITION*

They say that no one has seen it clearly till today
But like a virus, it can be anywhere
Whenever immunity is low, it catches hold
If someone runs away, a gunshot hits him on the back
If he stays still, a gunshot hits him on the forehead

Then comes the official statement:
No one has died, only a few people are missing
Then in the search for the missing people, many start to die
In the verandas of courts, secretariats, police stations, hospitals
In the fields and barns, in the prisons, in crowds,
Amid the springtime happiness of the majority
they fall with the falling leaves
The winds sweep them away into the universe

Even the judicial enquiry committee learns nothing
People begin to die in such a way
that they themselves don't know they have died
Dead men have no homes
Their own people refuse to recognize them
the way they refuse to recognize unclaimed bodies
They are expelled even from the footpaths
Everywhere everyone only asks them for their papers
Wives, children, neighbours, they all say: get your papers
The government, too, solaces: you're alive, just show your papers
Work, water, food, laughter: they forget everything else
and look only for their papers

But in their whole world, these papers can't be found anywhere
Tired, defeated, they come to believe they, with their family,
have died

**Translated from the Hindi by Annika Taneja.*

Then they themselves begin to say, We've been dead for centuries
We died in the womb itself, we have no papers
We are naturally dead, we have no papers
Our ancestors came to live on this earth before papers
They left a long time ago and they left no papers

The government says, We never kill anyone
We are simply enforcers of the law
Official deaths are a superstition; everyone dies their own death
The newspapers and the TV channels remind us of this
day and night.

ANAMIKA

is a Delhi-based Hindi poet, novelist, translator and associate professor of English. Poems from her national award-winning poetry collections—*Khurduri Hatheliyan, Doob-Dhan* and *Tokri Mein Digant*—are prescribed at national universities such as Jawaharlal Nehru University, SNDT University, Kochi University, and also at the University of Moscow. Her novels—*Dus Dwaare Ka Peenjara* and *Tinka Tinke Paas*—have been staged as major productions in Marathi and Malayalam. Along with her poems, her essays on womanist discourse in Hindi have been translated in languages such as Russian, French, Spanish, Norwegian, Punjabi, Bangla, Malayalam, Odia, Kannada and English. Her translations of Rilke, Neruda, Doris Lessing, Octavio Paz and fellow women poets have been published by the Sahitya Akademi, HarperCollins, Katha and Penguin. Her doctoral thesis is on John Donne and her major English publications include *Transplanting British Poetry in Indian Classrooms, Donne Criticism Down the Ages, Post-War Women Poets: Treatment of Love and Death, Feminist Poetics: Where Kingfishers Catch Fire, Translating Racial Memory, Weaving a Nation: Proto-Feminist Writing in Hindi and Urdu (1920-47)*. She is a trained Kathak dancer and has an MA and a PhD in Hindi too.

CRACKING THE LOCKOUT*

Though girls were not supposed to meet *aghories*,
At age ten I had met one
At a friend's place
Her father was a doctor.
Knocked down by his old Hillman car,
When the bleeding old *aghori* was brought home,
In pious protest
He hurled the choicest abuses.
Amidst all hue and cry
Something that he said
Stayed back

'If your world offers just no scope for life,
It must at least let one die with dignity,
To hell with your mad attempts to save me.
I was anyway going to die
With the dignity of an old serpent
Who somehow senses that his days are numbered
And then
Peacefully he hides in his hole
Just to let the energy dissipate by and by,
This is the way we all should die
As if we have disappeared from the surface of the earth
Without a sigh.'

Once again
The same hue and cry
As my country cousins—
The migrant labour from Bihar—
Are shown on the TV screen

---

* *Translated from the Hindi by the poet.*

Running back home,
Cracking the lockdown.
On foot they are rushing back
Quite like the hungry masses
After the Civil War in
The Grapes of Wrath
'Lock down? Who cares?
Home is a better place for falling dead
What if the walls have collapsed
And Baba's cot has given way!
What if in mother's hanging pot
Now pigeons lay their eggs!
I shall still fit in and die with grace.'
I can see the old *aghori*
In the boy's wrath.

O dear Kabir,
Excuse them please,
They have not yet mastered your advice—
'Fall dead in distant lands,
For vultures and worms to make merry and feast on your flesh.'
Against all risks
I can see them running on and on
Non-stop,
'Let the Coronavirus
Feast upon us,
It is better any day
Than to starve and fall dead in Pardes, the alien land.'
On and on they run
Till they go beyond
All confines of
Time and Place.

JOTAMARIO ARBELÁEZ

is a Latin American poet from Colombia. He is the main exponent of the Nadaísta movement, a group of rebellious poets and writers who revolutionized Colombian literature in the 1960s. He was one of the first followers of its founder, Gonzalo Arango. He has been awarded three national poetry prizes in Colombia and the Víctor Valera Mora International Prize from the Rómulo Gallegos Foundation in Caracas, Venezuela. The University of Zacatecas of Mexico and the Spanish Academy have awarded him with prizes for his work. He has represented Colombian culture in thirty-five countries, including India and China.

LET LIFE GO ON!

There is a picture window opposite the desk where I set out my jumbled mix of words,
giving out onto a range of blue mountains beneath a sky white with clouds,

Before the mountains rises green woodland, whose trees are hidden,
Alder, oak, pine and eucalyptus,
Covered in birdsong, where the sunlight peeks,
of goldfinches, blackbirds, nightingales and robins.

Dina and Leon, my two dogs, former strays, run wild up there,
barking at the thick-tailed squirrels as they scamper among the trees.

The sound of Bach drifts on the air.
My wife is listening to the Oboe Concertos as performed by Puskunigis and the St. Christopher Chamber Orchestra.

On the nightstand sits my copy of *Paradise Lost*,
where I left it in search of the blind man, Milton.

I have been careful not to bend my page to mark it,
Instead I use what they call an apple-paring knife.

I know that for several months a pandemic has been hovering above the earth,
halting all activity and threatening to put an end to the human race,

The authorities have decreed an indefinite period of quarantine,
that has brought the population to the brink of starvation, despair and even madness.

Never before has humanity been so caught out, governments helpless, ill-equipped with hospital beds or

ventilators, to care for the sick and dying, and hardly any
traffic over land, sea or air,
deprived of cultural or sporting events, breathing through
masks, and afraid even to choose the right floor in
the elevator, or press the doorbell.

'At least you caught AIDS by screwing,' complains
my muse Diana Merlini from her nursing home on San Andres.

With time to spare before continuing my *scherzo*, I take a walk
into the wood
thinking on how to finish it.

As descriptions of happiness are often tedious for the reader
and even
offensive to those who cannot bear to see the warrior at rest
above all if it is at home with a bar, a library and a
comfortable bed.
Turning eighty and listening to the bleating of the second
generation, offspring of my own disobedient gene.
'Our proletarian anarchist has turned bourgeois' is the most
restrained of all the criticism.

I see a girl approach with a basket and cheeks redder than her cap.
Around sixteen years old and with one shoe hanging off.
Smiling she holds out the basket to me.
I bend my knee to tie up her shoe but, thinking it could be a
trap laid by the Devil to make me fall into the
hands of the police or of Covid-19, I take a detour in search of
the stream where I bathe naked to calm my
troubled spirit.

On its bed I find a gold nugget the size of my wife's navel. She
prefers beads but I will make her a present of it.

Back in The Magic Mountain I take up my keyboard again like
a virtuoso.

The clouds have now parted, revealing scraps of lapis lazuli
sky, the birds are silent and my cell phone plays
Violin Concertos by Emmy Verhey and Antonio Luco
Camerata.

The under-gardener is hard at work weeding the lawn but the
dandelions will return.
Our maid Alejandra asks me if I prefer fruit juice or a
Margarita.

I take a bubble bath and my electric razor gives some shape to
my beard.
The aroma of vetiver makes me hold my head still higher.
Those hair implants are still growing.
I still cannot think of how to finish my article but I am in no
mood to ask God for help.

What is the point, when I know from the start that the tiniest
and most lethal speck,
from the country of my beloved Arancha Lou, has escaped

and is going to put an end to all human life,
even God, without someone to give him a face, will cease
to exist.

My telephone rings without disturbing the concerto.

*'Hello, poet, a voice says, this is Adolfo Vera Delgado speaking,
your chief cardiologist. I am calling to tell
you I read everything you write in the newspapers and on social
media. I want you to know that I am
concerned. In your most recent publications, you talk of death, and
of how you are close to death. This is not
healthy. I know you will tell me you are only joking, but I doubt the
Grim Reaper has a sense of humour. You
have a gift and you are writing like an angel. Now is not the time to
for you to join them. The last time I took*

your blood pressure and performed a thorough check-up of your heart I made a discovery. You will live to be ninety-six. So please my friend, change the subject. The world is not about to end, and life is beautiful.' He hangs up.

The world is not going to end and life is beautiful. That is all. This precious life and the unending world are writing for me.

ASMAA AZAIZEH

is a poet, essayist and cultural manager based in Haifa. In 2010, Asmaa received the Debutant Writer Award from Al Qattan Foundation for her volume of poetry, *Liwa* (2011, Alahlia). She has published two other volumes of poetry: *As the Woman from Lod Bore Me* (2015, Alahlia) and *Don't Believe Me if I Talk of War* (2019) in Arabic, Dutch and Swedish. Asmaa has also published a bilingual poetry anthology in German and Arabic, *Unturned Stone* (2017, Alahlia). She has contributed to various journals and anthologies, and participated in poetry festivals around the world. Her poems have been translated into English, German, French, Persian, Swedish, Spanish, Greek, and other languages. In 2012, Asmaa became the first director of the Mahmoud Darwish Museum in Ramallah. She has worked as a cultural editor in several newspapers, a presenter on TV and radio stations, and as the artistic director of the Fattoush gallery in Haifa where she had also set up an annual book fair.

READING BIOGRAPHIES OF PROPHETS*

I am a great admirer of the lives of prophets.
Reading them is like buying a lottery ticket:
the long fantasy they contain of a peaceful life,
perfectly empty.
So lost in thought you can hear God
whisper in your inner ear,
and you in turn mutter words unknown
to human invention.
You can see ultraviolet and infrared.
You speak the language of frogs.
You chase from your heart
all the anguish of mountains.
You rid the world of its habit
of eating its own waste.

Gentlemen, this is not a game,
not some trick to write a trifling poem,
not some ramble in a passing valley.
The prophets worked hard at it.
They saw so clearly their eyes dried up,
and they spoke the words that have not left our lips
for thousands of years.

I want to speak like them
but my imagination is the size of a mouse hole
and all its bright, quick mice
were found slaughtered at its door.
I want to say a word about slaughter,
about the slaughtered tents

** Translated from the Arabic by Yasmine Seale.*

in slaughtered lands.
About their residents,
who fell from their mothers
already slaughtered.
About the mothers, slaughtered
in warehouses and wells
like hens
with the knives of their children.

Gentlemen, this is not a game.
This is infrared and ultraviolet.
Even acid cannot touch it.
We must be prophets
and madmen to see it.
I want to say a word about my indifference
to the nation,
about my sadness and the way
it clashes with this age of springs
fabricating hope.
I do not fabricate hope.
I wash the brains of my friends
and I tell them this nation is the size of a mouse hole
and I drag them to the plane door.
I want to say a word about those who have no planes,
to whose doors they cannot be dragged,
and when they go out in search of one,
are slaughtered and return
on ice, like vegetables.

But I will say nothing
for my neck is short and I cannot see
the bottom of the well.
My life is nothing
but a looping line

between home and work
and back.

On my way I see girls
hopping onto buses
with the lightness of hens,
and lottery tickets darkening
the city skies,
and slaughtered prophets
pecked by flies.

DRAGONFLIES*

Millions of years ago, there were no winged creatures.
We all crawled around on our bellies and paws
to arrive.

We arrived nowhere in particular,
but the rough ground coarsened our bellies
and our paws stretched out like mountains.
Every time we stopped in the shade of a tree,
one of us would shout: 'Here we are!'
A fantasy mightier than mountains.

Millions of years ago, dragonflies emerged from narrow
streams.
The water was heavy on their backs,
like a tightening in the chest,
so they asked creation for wings,
that they might perceive anguish
as clearly as stones on the riverbed.

---

* *Translated from the Arabic by Yasmine Seale.*

Since then, we all fly,
millions of wings and planes cloud the sky,
humming like hungry locusts.
But not one of us has asked creation
to deliver us from the fantasy of arrival.
In our chests, the same tightening.

BRIEF WORDS FROM THE COFFIN*

The coffin is empty
the tulips on my belly unopened
I might as well die of boredom
the time has come
for me to utter
the words that had passed me by in life
Resting on my tongue is a pot-bellied bird
Fields of scarecrows that multiply in the image
of all the men I have known
Resting on my tongue
are tanks the war had left in my courtyard
because I had abstained from wallowing in its fire
and all these flayed words, which mourners had plucked away

My corpse will be washed by strange women
who will turn my heavy flesh around
and glimpse my three tattoos
they will imagine my body on fire under the earth
and pity me, chanting . . .
'The hereafter . . . the hereafter . . . the hereafter . . .'

---

* *Translated from the Arabic by Adam Zuabi.*

They will go out and shame me
'Crows the size of men gushed out of her holes
. . . bald crows . . . crows with their tongues cut . . .'

What afterlife, my dear stranger?
I am still busy with the previous,
I have not let go of it to die
I have not heard Gabriel's whistle,
not a trumpet's cry,
nor a resurrection resurrected
Love had slapped me when I was still
tracing the depressions it had left on my face
my sleep was still brimming,
I, my dear stranger, don't even lend my books,
so how can I lend my dreams?
I am still not done with collecting my favourite photos and
framing them
I will forget what they show If I don't see them
Your God will ask me: what have your hands made?
I will reply: I have no hands.
Strange women put a spell on me with strange water

I have not learnt all of life's lessons yet
I have not learnt how to heal the lame foot of my rancour
Or to hide from love's slap like a straw from a blaze
How to smell the corpses of those slaughtered in massacres
without mistaking it for mine
I have not learnt how to feed the dogs of defeat
Before they sink their teeth in my neck

The crows will bury me because like them
I have never learnt how to walk
I ran until I collided with a massacre
and broke my nose

The hand of the strange woman is cold
Her palm forever sprouting feathers and caws
and in the background my own voice
speaking words about boredom.

STANLEY H. BARKAN

is the editor/publisher of Cross-Cultural Communications that has produced approximately 450 book titles in fifty-nine languages. His own work has been translated into twenty-eight languages and published in twenty collections, several of them bilingual (Armenian, Bulgarian, Chinese, Dutch, Italian, Persian, Polish, Romanian, Russian, Sicilian, Spanish). His latest books include *As Yet Unborn* (2019), translated into Dutch by Germain Droogenbroodt; *Pumpernickel* (2019), translated into Persian by Sepideh Zamani; *From Rhythm to Form* (2019), complementary poetry with the paintings of Marsha Solomon.

AFTER THE FALL

After the flood,
the raven and the dove
made nesting places
on the moon.

After the rain
came down,
the craters' manna
made igneous the earth

the seas gathered
into Sargasso mists
and albatrosses hung
from every neck
of corpses straddled
on the naked trees.

After the plowshares
turned to swords
slicing at the wind,
the mustard seeds
burst into flaming vines.

After the fall,
the ape man and Lilith
danced macabre
in the valley
of the dragon's teeth.

SILENT DARK

When even the early sundreams
are shrouded behind
impenetrable clouds,
the starless nights endure
and morning
comes without a light,
like blindmen
we will stumble through
the lampless streets,
beneath blackened windows
opened without eyes
to greet our opened mouths,
our seeking hands.
The white of teeth
cannot reflect
when even moons
are vanished from the sky.
We will listen
for a voice
that will not speak,
Shriek out
in the silent dark
for even an echo
to resound within
some hidden ear
muted in the stillness
of a world
etched into the grey
of forgetfulness.

AMANDA BELL

is an award-winning Irish poet. Her publications include *First the Feathers* (Doire Press, 2017), *The Lost Library Book* (The Onslaught Press, 2017), *Undercurrents* (Alba Publishing, 2016) and *the loneliness of the sasquatch: a transcreation from the Irish of Gabriel Rosenstock* (Alba, 2018). She works as a freelance editor, specializing in poetry manuscripts. Amanda won the William Allingham Poetry Prize, was selected for Poetry Ireland's Introductions Series in 2016 and has been commended twice for the Patrick Kavanagh Award. Her work has been shortlisted for the Shine Strong Award for best first collection, a Touchstone Distinguished Books Award, and won a Kanterman Merit Book Award.

BUMBLEBEES

There was no need to fret about the bees—
their fragile nest, unlidded
as I pulled weeds beneath the apple tree,
their squirming larvae naked
to my gaze and to the sun.

They watched me from the border
while I hastily replaced the roof,
before returning to rethread
the fibres of their grassy home.

In the cleared weeds I see
their entrance and their exit,
how their flightpaths sweep
the garden in an arc, stitching up
the canvas of this space, as if
they could remake the world
which lies in shreds around us.

The dome moves, as I watch it,
the stretching of an inchoate form—
when morning comes
it glistens with white dew.

BUTTERCUPS

Buttercups spread overground as well as under—
runners take long leaps, bite down for purchase, leap again,
white clustered roots form galaxies below.

Fork-loosened soil admits my fingers—
I work them underneath and gently tug, then throw,

over my shoulder a mountain quickly grows,
of tangled green trajectories, tufted white nebulae.

The cleared soil is friable, beetle-riddled, rich—
there will again be beans, pebble-smooth potatoes,
stubborn beetroot, white-spined chard in rows.

The buttercups throw long green ropes,
dig-in winter camps.
In spring, their golden satellites
will signal to the sky.

The moon draws tides across the shifting globe—
seeds burst, seas die,
I'm throwing weeds over my shoulder,
they regroup just out of sight.

MAAZ BIN BILAL

is a writer, translator and academic, based in the national capital region of Delhi. He is the author of *Ghazalnama: Poems from Delhi, Belfast, and Urdu*. Maaz is also the translator of Fikr Taunsvi's *Chhata Darya or The Sixth River: A Journal from the Partition of India* from Urdu. His translation of Mirza Ghalib's Persian long poem on Banaras, *Chirag-i-Dair*, is forthcoming. Maaz was a Charles Wallace India Trust fellow in creative writing and translation, and teaches at Jindal Global University.

WHO DID IT?

The call of the lapwing sounds at night, 'who did it!'
On which detection must we alight, 'who did it?'

The whole town was witness to the crime, nonetheless,
the haakim forces the victim: 'Write—who did it!'

A plague is afoot, sifting through humanity,
Who spread it? Where'd it come? Is it not trite: who did it?

Where we go from here may scream to the skies
of the bravery of all those who fight who did it.

Nature's self-correction, the sins of the fathers,
Did a god will this to set aright who did it?

I am drunk on wine, and they are on power,
Who'll adjudge who is wrong, who is right, who did it?

The rich live in isolation in large bungalows,
Abdul, who built that house, must fight who did it.

Deserts of loneliness, and ghettoes and camps,
Who put them there and set them alight, who did it?

Birds still chirp, humour persists, there's laughter, oh, Maaz,
Do not write poetry from pain to spite who did it.

MAREN BODENSTEIN

is a South African writer of German descent. Leaping across forms, she has published a novel, children's stories, short stories, flash fiction and essays. She is working on a memoir that tries to untangle her female ancestors from the late nineteenth-century German Lutheran missionary culture they were born into. Maren has come to the pleasures of poetry only recently and an anthology is currently brewing.

THE HOWLS OF HEKATE

Howl
The moon is rising.
Breathe in, breathe out.
Beyond these walls
The sky is whistling softly,
It's calling you to fly the naked trees.
Dogs bark.
Your broken brothers
Creep around the garden,
They're snatching after gold.
Cold yellow night,
Your lungs are limp.
Breathe in, breathe out.
Your knife is blunt from scraping at the sky,
You can't get in.
You are enraged.
Howl
The moon is rising.

Hush
The sun has set.
Hold your breath
And fall
Towards the luscious ground
That sings to cats
Deep in their wilderness.
See, your sisters fly,
They're smearing blood
Across the dark-eyed sky.
Heart pumps.

Your fingers stroke the earth.

It laughs out loud

And opens up.

You slide inside.

Hush

The sun has set.

ANN BRACKEN

has authored two poetry collections, *No Barking in the Hallways: Poems from the Classroom* and *The Altar of Innocence*. She serves as a contributing editor for *Little Patuxent Review* and co-facilitates Wilde Readings Poetry Series in Columbia, MD. Her poetry, essays, and interviews have appeared in numerous anthologies and journals. Ann's advocacy work centres around arts-based interventions for mental health and prison reform.

THE IMPORTANCE OF FLOWERS

Rescuing a cluster of pink blossoms
lying next to the sidewalk,
I inhale my mother's silk scarf
and cradle the velvet petals.
Immediately
I am caught in the slipstream of time,
emerging as the little girl in a blue jumper
carrying a bouquet of fresh flowers.
That morning, my mother braved a thicket of spring grass
to snip forsythia and cut bunches of lily-of-the-valley.
She wrapped the flowers in waterlogged paper towels,
secured with wax paper and a loose rubber band.
I felt special that day, bringing flowers for Mary's altar
set up in the front of my fourth-grade classroom.

I cup the pink flowers in my palm
as carefully as I carried the Mary bouquet to school.
Inscribed in my memory, a soft-focus polaroid of the days
when the Hail Mary was a rote prayer
recited before every class
and the phrase 'now and at the hour of our death'
held no fear.

IN NEED OF IMAGINATION

I wake to the call of the warbler
another morning where the flame of inspiration
sputters under the intangible sense
that life has been suspended.
Preparing coffee feels fractious—
the pulse and whir of grinding beans
the tangle of electric cords
waiting for the day to begin
with toasting and blending and boiling.

My country wraps itself in hubris
despite bridges routinely collapsing.
Sunlight fractals on the brook.
I hold a leaf in my palm
hoping for an end to the unsparing
rigidity of the powerful.

GRACE CAVALIERI

is an American poet, playwright and radio host of *The Poet and the Poem* from the Library of Congress. Poet laureate of Maryland, Cavalieri has published several volumes of poetry. She has also written twenty-six plays and two operas that have been produced.

THE POET ACTS AS IF HER THOUGHTS ARE GOOD ENOUGH

Listening is how we learn to talk
to hear the train-whistles in the distance
of course in the distance
no tracks are here
I wonder where it's going
it's going home without you

Putting things back
so even the silence
in dreams vanishes
within earshot of the gods
what I will miss most of all
is that you were not here with me

Between mind and thought the moon in springtime
a candle of night
lighting the day
does the moon know it means
the end of the day
like the sound you never hear
as there are no footsteps behind me
as useless as the moon

Pain in the heart again here it is
lying on my side
something secret is all my own
visiting nightly
a splinter which cannot be removed
the fear that no one hears me
I love that feeling
because it is mine.

If I hold out my hand
and give you a key

no matter how far I reach
there is no one to lift the latch
beyond the door
there is no key no hand
and all that remains is
the air you wanted and
could not hold
the way I pretended
there was a key
and the door
and someone to open it.

DEAR WORD PRISONER

From here you can see the water past craggy purple
rocks, stretches of green, rusted roof tops,
limned fields—yet this is not enough—
Spirits need language and what does it matter
unless we can describe the outdoor air at dark,
the late-night owl or fox,
walls leaning thick with loss,
stones large with dirt and leaves and moss—
Many souls lived and walked here on their way to heaven.
What led them on, glittering with love of luck?
Tell me what world we can speak of if it is not this,
the roaring of the ocean,
the emptiness of winter's gate—
I've visited these places but left
for all the words that could not touch them.
Anything I say! Squeal, cry, yelp, sigh out loud,
say something, mouth, say summer,
talk of hands that held here. Whose?

The convert feathers rest silent in the tree
for lack of sound from heart.
Dear tongue, breath:
Don't leave me here alone with all this disappearing.

ISOLATION

At some point you will have to forget about being in all
those houses
different but the same with the neighbours singing songs all
around you
you always knew old friends were alive but now are only in
memory
the thought of memory
the people who knew something about you
you would not recognize them now and they may not recognize you
out the window I see a crane walking the fence
and seeing one mile over the water the tree hovers like a parasol
once, on the downtown brick stoop next to the wooden complex,
we sat and ate ice cream and listened to everyone before losing
the future
we played on the docks with the unborn and the now dead
where every street was a flag in the alphabet where we could
go all day
now the spaces are not there or else we're not there
or something is not as vivid as it should be or as comforting
with trees lined up and leaves stacked in piles outside
I could smell woodsmoke, you can still smell it if you imagine
in tune with the earth's breathing it was an illusion being outside
where is it now the past lets go of you as soon as you let go
this neighbourhood we thought we knew remains somewhere
somewhere without us.

SAMPURNA CHATTARJI

is a writer, translator and teacher. Her eighteen books include eight poetry titles, the most recent being *Space Gulliver: Chronicles of an Alien* (HarperCollins, 2015, 2020); *Elsewhere Where Else/ Lle Arall Ble Arall* (Poetrywala, 2018), co-authored with Eurig Salisbury; *Over and Under Ground in Paris & Mumbai* (Context, Westland Publications, 2018), the result of a collaboration with poet Karthika Naïr, illustrated by Joëlle Jolivet and Roshni Vyam. *Dirty Love* (Penguin, 2013) is her collection of short stories about Bombay/Mumbai. Her translation of Joy Goswami's *Selected Poems* is a Harper Perennial; and *Wordygurdyboom!*—her translation of Sukumar Ray—is a Puffin Classic. She is currently poetry editor of *The Indian Quarterly*.

NOTHING

I have been looking at nothing for days now
wondering when, at which unsprung moment,
it might engulf me so utterly
all utterance would be shallowed.

I succeeded in sweeping the verb away.

Dumped it in the backlot where the rubbish was burnt,
under the rain tree where the crows usher in the dawn
with their cacophonous claim:
now now now sluggard humans wake up!
it's morning now!
They scream blue murder at times, around two a.m.
when all the pi dogs join in—an untamed feline from the hills
is in their midst, they smell its jungle scent and are afraid,
so afraid, they want us sleeping mortals to wake, and take
their side
under the rain tree where the pigeons were fed the scattered
seed,
huge greedy flocks pecking till scattershot by pistol sound.

On that forsaken ground, I dropped the verb,
once claimed by vagrant children with bats under their arms
on this shortcut from nowhere to nowhere, place
of makeshift stages for events where no one comes,
no music louder than absence, occupying so much space
you never suspect that beyond the branches there aren't really
seven hundred young boys and girls clacking their sticks
and twirling their skirts in slow monotonous circles.

I only dared to look at nothing
after consigning doing to the dump.

Now, nothing is all I see.

I look and look and when I find myself falling headfirst
I know nothing can stop me now
this vertiginous descent is written into my vertebrae
I shall not crack my head open when I hit bottom
because nothing is bottomless
and I have found my wayward feet
and finally learnt to dance.

JUST THINK, WHEN YOU ARE CURED

Collapsed lung / Child / An unusual opacity in the left lung
Kidney removed / Small Bowel Follow Through
Elbow dislocation / Angiogram hand
Lung details disappeared / No air

Coral blooming inside bodies / nocturnal and malignantly
hushed
Pinned down / by neat arrows and labels
In that / black and white place of Dread
You are in Michigan / I in Mumbai / In seconds
You will come to me / fractured bent distended
The merciless eyes / of the beast in the radiologist's machine
It is the beginning of healing / to know what is wrong
I will not let it crush me / pump me breathless / bellowing

Your wrist is adorable / a bracelet of bone
The northern lights blaze / in your lung
Just think / when you are cured / we will marvel
At how pretty they are / those pictures of the country
We carry inside ourselves / Just think
Of the joy of returning / to that heedlessness
That enormous ingratitude of the well / But until then

Until then / picture me counting
One to thirty-seven / each second twisting down the phone line
Like an absurd postponement / of pain

Living is a kind of mourning too
To hold what the dead have lost

NISHI CHAWLA

is an academician and a writer. She has six collections of poetry, nine plays, two screenplays and two novels to her credit. She has also written, directed and produced her first movie, *Mixed Up*, a story about interracial love. The movie will be completed by Fall 2020. She holds a PhD in English from George Washington University, Washington, D.C. After nearly twenty years as a tenured professor of English at Delhi University, India, she migrated with her family to a suburb of Washington D.C. She taught at the University of Maryland from 1999 until 2014. She is now on the faculty of Thomas Edison State University, New Jersey.

INSIDE MYSELF

The virus licks my torn soul, guilt tripping me,
I sing a love song to it, tempting the faint thump,
Causing my heart to fissure its fatty lumps; pretend
I live on a moon of my own landing, turn my flesh
Inside out, listen to the chirping of birds, amazed.

That so much beauty could still exist, amid club-like
Spikes that crush the breathing soul, lavender storms
That hit, unfounded hopes cluster phylogenetically;
A pestilence that asks for enormous surcharges, lethal
As the protean cry of daggers, stabbing me yet again.

Quietly slithering out, a warlike stratagem, as
Birds orchestrate their cheerful songs to each other,
Embraced in positive sense RNA, the hard truths that
No flowers on our windowsills would relive. Proteins
That slice human voices, sliced lungs pause, then breathe.

When I follow its replication pattern, somewhere
A flood of tears ensue, attached to a host receptor, slyly
Pursuing a purpose-driven path, winter turns into stunned
Spring, and yet the stalk of the spike molecules sticks,
Digs deep within, encodes hollow dreams, hollowed out.

In the open fields, the birds shriek with intense,
Tormented sounds, adopt a transmembrane-like structure,
And more and more are rendered mute, transfixed fear,
Packaging signals of sliding down, motionless companions
That express a fear; triggering viral particles, spreading out.

Binding domains of dazed displeasure, disbelief,
A tissue culture, receptors and protein that inject so much,
A solar vision that gives me a new calm, a prayer that

Sparks nucleocapsids of refined pleasure,
Gone, I struggle with myself again, umpteen times more.

INFINITE KARMAS

At the beginning was the outbreak,
Blobs of swarming virus caught red-handed,
Fasten themselves on human lungs, above those
Karmic laws that got bled out; the stars rip, the
Effects of human intention, strayed, swelled.

How one lives, front-lined with gloves and masks,
Mock at causality, casually proliferate in
Invisible tweets, with red mountain clouds,
Dismantle the short supply of legends that
Look us in the eye, comfort us for no reason.

Does it clink a glass or two, now that the karmic
Wheel got broken? Does it dodge bullets, whittled
By the dark scraping, bend its shapes, inside the
Deep flesh in cruel thumps, knowing no clear
Patterns of reactionary consequences? Pacing

Oneself to match an invisible fugue-like enemy
That rings in waves of new energy, in unison
With the crevices the virus revisits;
Wild affliction, dead to the pangs of love, of
Lust, reaping the aroused days of its own self.

Karma-scapic bounds, where is the blind eye
Of fate here, discriminate between willing it
Nor etched, nor accrued, in discrete scoops, shields

Of our own actions, generating, flourishing,
Between the responsible and not so?

MUTATING

At the turn of a metaphor, an old
Smell returns. Doorknobs, food parcels,
Cardboard boxes violate its safety.

Coffins run amuck, unwilling to settle
Into the ground of unequal notes, broken up
Handshaking that combines data distancing.

By sunrise, singing, widows cut open fear,
From the clinging smell of soaps, to peacetime
Talk of floating civil liberties, affixed, then ripped.

Destroy the game of winners and losers, write
Love poems to battles fought, tactile as panic,
Controlled eyes lifting, glisten with godhead.

Its rhetoric is framed, unstable as molecules,
Moving, evolving, thinking unto oneself, deadly
And pent up, galvanized into action, fight, fleeing.

Quiver with soft gestures, smoothed out as dream
Filaments, the laboured action of digital steps, quiet
Lingering gestures, sinking deep, as surveillance.

As a door shuts tight, breathing encircled, then
intervene with the arc of biometrics, move freely
Between borders, strike back torrents of smart bombs.

Creep into bunker busters, masked under submarines,
Guns that manoeuvre through host cells, a blood flow
Bereft of motion, would there be a mutating stir?

MARIUS CHELARU

is a Romanian poet from Iaşi, Romania. He has published over forty books, including novels, poetry, literary criticism, essays and translations. He is a member of several national and international professional associations, including the Writers' Union of Romania, the World Haiku Association in Japan, and the Romanian Language Writers' Union of Quebec.

LOVE DURING QUARANTINE*

The town breathes fear
the moon hides behind the clouds
the people behind the walls
the streets are enveloped in the dark
the words have hidden *in former times*
the oppressive air hides hope

for a while
we have been together
two thoughts
cracked by the times
at their margins

the worm of silence grows
the walls between them are like our palms

alone
separated
we appear at the window
the town is darker than the night

from your eyelashes
older tears run to me
from a glass of loneliness drunk by you and me

I feel your heart quiver
I caress you and wipe the fright from your face

when the moon drives away the clouds from her eyes
spreading light upon us
we already kiss

from another window
someone begins singing a love song

** Translated from the Romanian by Olimpia Iacob and Jim Kacian.*

suddenly the town
is a large singing heart
the air
a fresh orchard under the rain's palms
when the song dies
there remains the light within us

it smells of silence so beautiful

THE OLD MAN AND SILENCE*

*(for E.D., survivor of communist prisons, of the Pitești experiment,** of the Golden Epoch,*** forced to his knees by loneliness and helplessness, at ninety-eight years, by COVID-19, by other people's fear, isolation and indifference.)*

he and death have stayed face to face for two days
he carefully thinks about it near the phone

he knows that his days are no longer as many as before

the books on the shelves caress his sadness with their titles
they, with him, listen to the silence that comes from nowhere

the wind receives the letters for the whole town
an infected postman has left them scattered on the pavement

it is night in all the houses in the streets and recesses
the people sunken in heavy silence have covered themselves
with fear

two abandoned kittens sleep soundly
and also the stones in the pavement

---

* *Translated from the Romanian by Olimpia Iacob and Jim Kacian.*

**One of the most sadistic experiments from communist prisons in Romania, based on torture, 'reeducation', starvation and murder.

***The name given by communist propaganda to that period when Ceaușescu was leader of Romania.

the moon plays with the thistle lost among the blocks of flats
and transplanted in several footsteps covered with dust
beyond the street two deserted counters
make the prices known to no one

he cannot rise to his feet to see the sky
but he has all the stars hanging from the sky of his memories

he stroked their intense light looking like caramel
or a scar because of the cold
he feels time that slowly embraces him
as if it were a transient friend saying goodbye

he curiously opens the Bible—is there anything written in it
about this apocalypse?
'What has been will be again, what has been done will be
done again;

there is nothing new under the sun.'

he smiles somehow gladly to the dark which
like some strange heat covers the room with shadows
he has touched the phone,
dead with silence, and remembers about detention
he quietly walks to tortures, thinking, 'God is everywhere'

could He be present even now in the souls of the people,
some running away from others
some dressed in cynicism and indifference?

he has fallen asleep, reconciled, stroking the phone
if all goes well, he might get rid of silence tomorrow

R. CHERAN

is a Tamil-Canadian academic, poet, playwright and journalist. He is a professor at the University of Windsor in Canada. He has authored over fifteen books in Tamil, and his work has been translated into twenty languages, including Malayalam, Telugu, Kannada and Bengali. Several volumes of his work have been published in English translation, including *In a Time of Burning* (Arc Publications, UK).

WATER LAMP*

Nine minutes.
We light thousands upon thousands of akal** lamps
Yet the waves refuse to rise.

From soil and from household niche
Rising up
Blue smoke prevails over light.

Attended by the grace of prayer
and the gods' desires,
The places they journeyed, the places they glowed,
The lands they lit on
Would be earth sanctified, untouched by contagion.
So it is believed.

They do not alight
Upon the houses, the nations, the palaces
Of believers.

Upon streets of sorrow,
Where the desert stretches out,
In refugee camps,
Where everyone smells the sweat
Of everyone,
Upon mosques,
Upon the last wishes of black bodies cast out
From infirmaries made impotent,
Upon oceans devoid of fish,
They alight.

Lamps that burn on water.

---

*Translated from the Tamil by Nedra Rodrigo.
**In Tamil, *'akal vilakku'* refers to a small clay or metal lamp, but the word 'akal' also means to distance.

YIORGOS CHOULIARAS

is a Greek poet, essayist, fiction writer and translator. In 2014, he was awarded an Academy of Athens prize for his innovative writing and his work in its entirety. His published books include *Iconoclasm* (1972), *Roads of Ink* (2005) and *Dictionary of Memories* (2013). His poetry has been published in translation in major periodicals and anthologies, including *Harvard Review, The Iowa Review, Ploughshares, Poetry, World Literature Today* and *Modern European Poets*, and in Bulgaria, Croatia, France, Italy, Japan, Lithuania, Romania, Sweden and Turkey, among other countries. Born in Thessaloniki, he studied and worked mostly in New York, before returning to Athens from Dublin. He has worked as a university lecturer, advisor to international cultural institutions, and as a correspondent and press counsellor at Greek embassies. He has been elected president of the Hellenic Authors' Society, the principal association of Greek literary writers.

WHAT I KNOW IS WHAT I DO NOT KNOW*

what I know is what I do not know
if that which I have forgotten I constantly remember
if every life reminds me of death
even if I don't know as I do know how to keep alive
the dead so that they can remember us

DON'T**

I don't write to you, I don't remember you, I don't forget
I do not destroy your letters
I do not want you to know where I am
I don't want you to ignore that I am away from you

THE OLDEST PROFESSION***

Death is a whore
who takes everyone

---

*Translated from the Greek by the author.
**Translated from the Greek by David Mason and the author.
***Translated from the Greek by David Mason and the author.

FRANCIS COMBES

is a French poet who has published thirty books of poetry. He is also a respected French translator of the poetry of Heinrich Heine, Bertolt Brecht, Vladimir Mayakovsky and Attila József. His poems have been translated into more than ten languages. He has also been the organizer of a campaign of poetry posters in the Paris metro, and that has contributed to a revival of poetry in France. He was in charge of the International Poetry Festival of Val-de-Marne, near Paris, for several years. He is now involved in the coordinating committee of the World Poetry Movement.

THE BIG BREAKDOWN*

When, after several weeks, everything had stopped
all around the Earth,
suddenly, it appeared clearly
the sky could be blue,
lives matter more than money,
and among all the commodities we produce
some are useless
and for the necessary ones
two or three hours' work a day is enough
and we'd better give
everyone what's necessary to live
and take care of what's actually important:
love, children, life, poetry . . .

When everything had stopped
during several weeks
It became clear, that, all around the Earth
there was but one sea,
one atmosphere
one mankind.

---

* *Translated from the French by Alexis Bernaut.*

EVENING PEACE*

What time is it in our lives?

This we do not know
as we'd rather go without a watch

Tonight, the setting sun
strokes the grass the right way
polishing it

By the wave of a magic wand the sun
in the meadow multiplies
its dandelion children

Tonight the sky will see
the pink moon rise

I can't say I'm worried
for nature after us

I'd rather worry for us.

* *Translated from the French by Alexis Bernaut.*

MICHAEL COPE

is a South African poet and novelist. His father was the distinguished novelist, Jack Cope. In addition to being a poet, he works as a writer, designer and goldsmith. His poetry collections, *Scenes and Visions* and *GHAAP: Sonnets from The Northern Cape*, deal with environmental issues and human origins.

FLOW

Relaxed in the flow of things, we float
Down the wide river in a small boat.
There is nothing to do but to pluck
With leisured fingers on the lute,
Let the song rise in the throat
And spill over the water, or not.

The boat drifts slowly. On either side
The landscape passes like a long scroll
Full of intricate detail. Each tributary's slide
Into the main stream makes the wide
River wider. How gradually we glide
Seawards, how vivid the afternoon sky.

The different water-birds around us
Vanish and return to the surface,
Drops sparkling. They are full of business
But we are caught up with luxurious
Late-day warmth, the lute idly plucked,
The possibility of a kiss.

Far over the river sounds can be heard:
A bull bellowing from his pen,
The high *chaa chaa* of a gliding water-bird
And the hint of the water's gurgle
Against distant banks. The returning herd
Answers the bull. The boat drifts on.

Six plums tied in a cloth, some bread,
Are all our simple provisions,
Along with half a bottle of cheap red.
All day we have followed the delicate thread
Of the lute. We glide and sing. Ahead
The huge moon rising, almost red.

All day we drifted downriver in our flimsy boat,
The dark cargo ships slid by like dreams.
Now we are beyond the delta. We float
On calm water, deep blue and remote.
There is no land beyond the wet
Horizon. The stars are coming out.

WAVE

What is it to see the wave-front coming?
What is it to say we're all in trouble?
What is it to say that when the bubble
Bursts, we'll fall poor-first into the humming
Dark and there'll be scarce loot in the rubble?
What is it to feel the front of the nearing blaze?

Why is it that we turn away?
Is it because the day is too long?
Is it we feel we are not strong
Enough to look that way?
Is it that the feel of looking's wrong
And we'd rather remain in the daze?

How high is the crest of the wave?
Is it brown with ooze or blue,
Or of a deeper hue?
Do we wonder what we can save
In its face, grasp at a few
Random things, or do we look away?

Why has the tide gone out so far
And so suddenly?

Why do the elephants break free
From their chains, and charge
Off among the high trees?

MANGALESH DABRAL

was born in 1948 in village Kaphalpani, Uttarakhand. He has published six books of poems, three collections of literary essays and sociocultural commentary, a book of conversations, two travelogues and a selection of English translation of poems, *This Number Does Not Exist*, published by Poetrywala, Mumbai, and BOA Editions, Rochester, NY. A widely translated poet, he has been a fellow of the International Writing Program at the University of Iowa in 1991. He has received numerous awards, including the Shamsher Sammaan (1995), the Pahal Sammaan (1998) and the Sahitya Akademi Award (2000) for his poetry book *Hum Jo Dekhte Hain*. Dabral has participated in a number of international poetry events, including The Poetry International Festival, Rotterdam, in 2008, and the Struga Poetry Evenings, Macedonia, in 2020. He has also translated Arundhati Roy's novel *The Ministry of Utmost Happiness* into Hindi. One of his poems is engraved at the main gates of the city centre in Eislingen, Germany. Dabral works as a cultural journalist and lives in Delhi NCR.

THESE TIMES*

Those who cannot see
cannot make out their way
Those who are crippled
cannot reach anywhere
Those who are deaf
cannot listen to life's footfalls
The homeless don't build a home
Those who are mad wouldn't know
what they want

These are such times
when anybody can turn blind crippled
deaf homeless mad.

TOUCH**

Touch the things that are kept on the table in front of you
Clock pen-stand an old letter
Idol of Buddha Bertolt Brecht and Che Guevara's photos
Open the drawer and touch its old sadness
Touch a blank sheet of paper with the words' fingers
Touch like a pebble the still water of a van Gogh painting***
Starting life's hullabaloo in it
Touch your forehead and hold it for a long while without
feeling shame

---

*Translated from the Hindi by Sarabjeet Garcha.

**Translated from the Hindi by Sudeep Sen.

***Reference to the Japanese film-maker Akira Kurosawa's film on Vincent van Gogh.

To touch it isn't necessary for someone to sit close
It is possible to touch even from very far
Like a bird from a distance who keeps her eggs protected

'Please do not touch' or 'Touching is prohibited'—don't believe
in such phrases
These are long-running conspiracies
Religious gurus holding flags, wearing crowns and shawls
Bomb-throwers, war-raisers indulge in for keeping us apart
The more dirt the more waste they spit
Only by touch can they be cleansed
Touch you must even though it turns things topsy-turvy

Don't touch the way gods priests bigots devotees disciples
Touch each other's feet and heads
Rather touch the way the tall grass appears to caress the moon
and stars
Go inward feel the moist spot touch
See if it still remains there or not in these ruthless times.

CYRIL DABYDEEN

is a Guyana-born Canadian writer of Indian descent. Along with several poetry collections, his recent books include *My Undiscovered Country, God's Spider, My Multi-Ethnic Friends and Other Stories*, and the anthology, *Beyond Sangre Grande: Caribbean Writing Today*. His novel, *Drums of My Flesh* (Mawenzie House, Toronto), won the top Guyana Prize for fiction and had been nominated for the IMPAC Dublin Prize. Cyril's work has appeared in over sixty literary journals and anthologies, including *Poetry, Prairie Schooner, The Critical Quarterly* and *Canadian Literature*. He is a former Poet Laureate of Ottawa (1984-87). He taught creative writing at the University of Ottawa for many years.

HEART AND LUNGS

The air we breathe is what the lungs
know about, what the ancient Greeks
or the Pharaohs contemplated best
more than Harvey of blood circulation.

Oh the heart and knowing what else
the rib cage tells us about, a distinct
rhythm only I will contend with,
like Odysseus, or some other

I've considered less about at
odd moments in distant places,
the imagination indeed, or being
Homer again with mythology.

Ithaca I will aim for, returning
home where I consider brain cells
and start humming to myself
about the liver, kidneys, spleen;

and veins, arteries, aorta, the alveoli,
bronchial tubes as I breathe harder
making sure I'm one step closer
to my own creative self, I know,

but resorting to valves; and those
who will come after with gadgets,
a doctor's tools yet hanging around
the neck I will again dwell upon

in my own way with a mighty
heave, not unlike real drama
played out on stage, blood-lust
being tragedy from the start.

ODE TO HIPPOCRATES

Who's Hippocrates, I know,
in Crete or someplace else—
calling out to the Sirens,
the Sea's own and asking you
for healing ways, the mind
or spirit's, not the body's own.
Oh, the body, and being with
Odysseus again but only with
Titans and Poseidon where all
life comes from underwater
close to a billion nerve cells,
globules, arteries and alveoli
I want you to know about
with an electron microscope—
pulse-beats really.
A magnifying glass, or what
else I must consider best, if
it is art's longing you see,
or medicine's ways it will be
with a stethoscope in hand—
a talisman hanging around
my neck, but not knowing
what's beating in the brain
as nothing's undone when
waves appear on the computer
screen, real art displayed:
a miracle I hear you say—
the heart beating stronger,
the aorta most of all, being
again in the Aegean Sea.

MUSTANSIR DALVI

is an Anglophone Indian poet, translator and editor. He has authored two books of poems in English, *Brouhahas of Cocks* and *Cosmopolitician*. His 2012 English translation of Muhammad Iqbal's *Shikwa* and *Jawaab-e-Shikwa*, as *Taking Issue and Allah's Answer* (Penguin Classics), has been described as 'insolent and heretical'. He is the editor of *Man without a Navel*, a collection of translations of Hemant Divate's poems from Marathi.

MY ROOM

1

The fifteenth coat of gold
on the granite crag satisfies me.
It is done, put in place.

The concrete tray has seven hundred
and seventy-eight stones.
I add this last one, my epitaph.

This stone is the largest.
The inscription,
fifteen patches of gold, made one.

A spotlight picks up the gold.
The epitaph glows,
but not overtly so.

Look upon the elements of my life:
my epitaph flashes messages
in golden Morse.

The stones are keys.
Each tells of where I found it,
never more than one from any one place.

2

I sleep on a sea of ochre.

On carpets, stretched taut,
wall to wall. They press
into my skin, make marks

that ripple and wave.
Sometimes, I twist and turn.
The ripples crosshatch.

All carpets end at walls
plastered in cow dung.
Walls are cool,

you can rest against them.
They turn warm in light
that you can read by.

The walls are soft to touch.
You can still see marks left
by bristles of a wet brush.

This is the confirmation of the wall
when it dries, its final words.
I read them, over and over.

The walls dampen words
to whispers.
Here, we rarely speak.

3

There are no greens in my room.
If you want any, come dressed in green.
Then my room welcomes you.

So do I. You go well with the stones.

My room has one window.
It is narrow and it is tall,
divided four ways by sashes.

Outside, you can see half a tree.

You get four views of half a tree.
You can look at them together,
or one by one. They don't object.

Sometimes, the branches swing.

I can't hear the sounds outside.

I play music to the dipping of branches.

It cleans my room of clutter.

4

My window faces east. That is not my doing.

Each morning the sun comes through.

Four rays enter the room.

Three are damped in ochre,

the fourth reflects off

the patch of gold on my epitaph.

This wakes me, gently.

My epitaph is also my alarm clock.

KINTSUKUROI

I have never believed poetry heals
but words can be birdlime
that keep the bricks of our fragilities in place.

I wonder Ghalib, could you not have reassembled
the shattered shards of your heart
rather than run to replace it from the bazaar?

Could you not have chosen instead
to glue the pieces with your felicity? Were you afraid
of amending rather than mending your beating chalice?

Did you not trust the lacquer of your verse
to hold it all together, like it does those
who hold your diwan as a bulwark to their lives?

Your words are brickbats to the enraged and marble
to those whose ardour needs cooling. My name is mud—
gold runs in my veins, grouting an imperfect dam that holds.

KEKI
N. DARUWALLA

is a major Indian poet in English. He has written over twelve books. He received the Sahitya Akademi Award in 1984 for his poetry collection, *The Keeper of the Dead*. His *Collected Poems (1970-2005)* was published by Penguin Books in 2006. He has also won the Commonwealth Poetry Award. His works of fiction include the novels *For Pepper and Christ*, *Ancestral Affairs* and *Swerving to Solitude: Letters to Mama*, and the collection of stories, *The Minister for Permanent Unrest and Other Stories*.

PROLOGUE TO THE SONNETS

The Devil never left Black Death in the foyer
to be discussed at length in devastating detail.
Cleverer than Satan and Iblis, those soul-sawyers
he couldn't ever fail!

He checked out of Hilton, memory had him dismayed:
Didn't the hotel echo some rhymester of yore?
Yes of course the guy who needed Hearing Aids,
his verse sonorous as a river gorge!

Having planted Brexit, the Devil thought of exits
make a run for it, though sad to leave Hilton,
in poor English he said, 'this place is truly gala'.

His task severe, bury memories of Black Death
in some catafalque, beyond the reach
of sonneteering bums like Daruwalla.

2

The boats don't keel as they unload their cargo
and the black death which has no nameplate yet,
clambers up Europe's back; the Fates, hard put to watch
its moves, have sin on their minds and redemption;
can cuirass, crown, a monk's cowl save a soul?
'They're all mashed up here, your fucking Highnesses
from Greek shithouses, naked corpses,
we gondoliers wouldn't know who is who?'

A friar shouts 'wash the sickness down the sea'
till he is scythed himself. Nations outlaw
coffin, cerements, shroud, or was it plague that did it?

The Cardinal hands over a year's hard labour
for the crime.
The scribbler asks, what have I done my Lord?
'You dared write a sonnet without a rhyme!'

BLACK DEATH

1*
The summons were from the Byzantium court,
he was wanted there, the king's son was dead,
the advance guard of buboes had got to him.
How did he take it? he asked. The king's eyes bled,

the messenger answered. Isaac, coiner and scribe
tried to address the king in that ornate hall,
but hysteria ruled, courtiers screamed, 'the Tartars,
stricken with disease threw plague across the wall,'

'they catapulted corpses into the city.'
The royal ribs withstood a shudder, 'think of Kaffa,
that Genoese port, not terror but think of pity

Leave witches alone, and their ghastly spells,
and keep the Jews away, they've suffered enough,
and no, they haven't put poison in our wells.

2
Reports from the sea crowd my dreams, winds seethe
with salt and fear; this could have been a jest
in old days, a threat from rat and flea, but now
this line of rodents, themselves fleeing the pest

---

*King of Byzantium, John VI Kantakou Zenos, lost his son, aged thirteen, to the plague.

frightens my court. Doctors tell us, the ones
in shining belts, with faces grey as sand,
rats are the invading army of the plague,
buboes their night camps on our dying glands,

which burn like cinders in the armpits, tough to view.
Why have heavens cursed us, the victims shout,
those still left with some spark in their sinew.

They did it, the court says, beggar, witch, Jew
and migrants; were there minaret and dome
dusk-lit, they'd have blamed it on mosques aglow.

3

How did we falter, my queen asks, tongue timorous
as it steps out from her just withered face.
Were defilers aboard in our kingdom, blasphemers?
Did usurers have a free run of the market place?

Has your executioner taken leave of his axe?
'He's dead my lady, of the disease.' 'And during Lent
did the peasantry fast with us?' 'Some were lax,
but our kingdom's no longer a divine instrument.'
'Whose wrath have we incurred then, some scullion's
from Devil's kitchen, or an enraged spark divine?'
'Wife, too many heresies around, trackers of bad smells,
gluttons for good beef but guzzlers of bad wine.'

Like a boiling stream cutting through hell
the plague moves on; for death it is harvest time!
Who dies tomorrow, only rodents can tell.

4

Doubt doesn't clear the brain but corrodes.
    the future, will it float?

Or go down? The coming years are bands across the eyes.
No black sails flare with dark omens on the boats

As the fleet from Black Sea moves into Messina
with rodents draped in flea and flea bites that bleed,
what is the bird-liver reader doing here?
What on earth is there left to read?

Night, no Lord's prayer comes in dream; some hear
tambourines!
Only the clatter of hooves on cobblestones,
as a skeleton rides a horse, must be quite a scene(!)

and women have seen fire in a dead man's bones
instead of marrow   the Queen
closes the door of dreams in sorrow.

5

The Cardinal from Venice

[A pilgrim to Jerusalem, the Cardinal
Drops by. Queen kisses his ring.
He offers his limp hand to me.
I ain't gonna kiss no such thing]

He starts with souls dying without absolution.
'This nightlong traffic isn't going well.'
He shakes his locks 'no penitence, no confession,
The spirit in agony hissing away to hell.'

'What of the stricken?' I ask, 'shillings as they clink
In the armpit? Why so bogged down with the soul?
We need doctors more than priests, don't you think?'
My queen looks at me, her eyes burning coals.

He changes track. 'The entire order will be upset
The Holy church itself could be facing blight.

It's an end to serfdom, footmen, scullions
will question authority—they'll ask for rights!'

He waves his arms. 'When will all this be curbed?'
'There's no salve,' I answer, 'but Time is herb.'

NAJWAN DARWISH

was born in Jerusalem, Palestine. He has been described as 'one of the foremost Arabic-language poets of his generation' (*The New York Review of Books*). Since the publication of his first collection in 2000, his poetry has been translated into more than twenty languages. Besides being a prominent poet, Darwish is a leading cultural editor in the Arab world. He has played an important role in developing Arabic cultural journalism by co-founding independent magazines and mainstream daily newspapers.

A SHORT STORY ABOUT THE CLOSING OF THE SEA*

When you turn down that street at the city's edge,
the one that leads to the camp,
if you see children leaving that school that resembles a prison,
if you see seven of them standing there, on the threshold of
silence, and watching,
if you see a slender child whose eyes are gleaming with all the
world's promises,
you'll have found my friend Tayseer.
His family has a country that was stolen in broad daylight,
and you can see the vigilance of its birds in his anxious eyes.
The cement houses,
the memories of tin sheets,
the voices that were fearful
of the occupying army's transceivers
through the long weeks of curfew—
none of this has taken the slightest spark from his eyes.
He saw the sea once, and nothing can convince him
he won't see it again.
'When the curfew's lifted, we'll take you to the sea'—
that's how they used to comfort him.
And when the curfew finally *was* lifted one evening, they said,
'The sea's closed now, go to sleep.'
He didn't sleep that night. He imagined an old man
who closed the sea by lowering a massive tin sheet that
stretched from the star on the horizon to the sand on
the shore:
the man secured it with a huge padlock,
then went back to his home (the padlock was larger

---

* *Translated from the Arabic by Kareem James Abu-Zeid.*

than the one on Tayseer's father's shop on Omar Mukhtar
Street).

When you walk down that street at the city's edge
(the one that leads to the camp),
if you see two eyes gleaming with all the world's promises,
ask them, I beg you, if the Gaza Sea has 'opened' yet,
or if it's still closed.

THE LAST MASK*

I haven't found it
yet:
the writing that liberates,
that I once grabbed hold of, floundering in those suburbs,
the writing that resembles passion
and youth
and the delights of the flesh
in the way it surprises.

I haven't found it
and maybe I'll stop looking, for I'm busy with trifles—
my knife is dull now, and I'm pretending
I have no time to sharpen it.

Time put on its masks and called to me
from behind the new-born in the cradle,
the infant on all fours,
the child's first steps,
the stumbling adolescent,
the misgivings of the youth,

---

* *Translated from the Arabic by Kareem James Abu-Zeid.*

and the grown man's despair.
Time called to me
from behind all the frail and aging promises
when time has no more masks to wear.

But now
I've got to crawl and walk and stumble forward
and chase down my misgivings
and precede all the promises
as I stretch myself out in the coffin.

The last mask is in my hands
and I must wear it now.

SANJUKTA DASGUPTA

is a poet, critic and translator from India. She is the recipient of numerous national and international grants and fellowships and has lectured, taught and read her poems in India, Europe, the US and Australia. She was the chairperson of the Commonwealth Writers Prize, United Kingdom. She is a member of the general council of the Sahitya Akademi and convener of its English advisory board. Sanjukta Dasgupta's published books include *Snapshots, Dilemma, First Language, More Light, Lakshmi Unbound* and *Sita's Sisters*. She has served as dean, Faculty of Arts, and professor, Department of English, Calcutta University.

WALKING HOME

Suddenly thousands and thousands
Of them became homeless
Who asked the migrant workers
To return to their native places?
Did they walk out or did they have to walk out
No one knows no one asks

No work, their on-site homes
Had to be emptied at once
No electricity, no water, no food, no money
The 'Attention Men at Work' signboards
Lay in the dust.

The many men, many women, many children
Just walked down roads and highways
All transport stood like statutes
As they walked past the buses, trucks, trains
No one asked them to stay at home during lockdown
They were turned out of their makeshift homes
As they could not work from home.

Those who stayed indoors during the lockdown
Walked on tread mills, jogged on balconies
Saw pristine river waters flowing effluent-free
Bird calls, peacocks on highways, a racing deer
Green grass, green trees, blue skies, sighting of
The snowy peaks and the sound of relative silence
Bonding with family, playing with children, watching TV
Movies, web series, video games, rarely books
Many spoke of kitchen work, gym at home, yoga and aerobics
And the routine sport of violent domestic spat.

While outside their sliding glass windows,
Outside their air-conditioned homes

The spectre of hunger stalked the jobless workers walking home
Half-fed, unfed, sizzled by the fury of the tropical summer
They are still walking towards the shelter called home
This free shelter called home is their only refuge.

Their tired footsteps
Echoed like drumbeats in the heart
Their vacant, hurt eyes, parched lips ask
'M'Lord
Are we citizens
Or are we refugees
In our own country?'

UTTARAN DAS GUPTA

is a New Delhi-based writer and journalist. His first novel, *Ritual*, was published in February 2020. He has also published a book of poems, *Visceral Metropolis* (Red River, New Delhi, 2017). He has worked as a journalist with *Business Standard* in New Delhi, and writes a column on cinema (*Frames per Second*) and on poetry (*Verse Affairs*). His second novel, *Inclement Clime*, is ready for publication. He teaches journalism at O.P. Jindal Global University in Sonipat, India.

BURIALS

For many nights,
I dream her
being buried—

only the cemetery changes:

a tropical forest
lush moss, berried undergrowth
with *drongos* singing

a stretch of a rocky beach
—the diggers impotent
against the black frozen sand,
mourners impatient with rigors
of bereavement

a windswept grassland—
pollen-heavy, too bright
they bring coffins slung from saddles of horses

a New Orleans send-off
they sing a McCartney number—trumpets, choruses

'I wish the world was ending tomorrow,'
he wrote.
'Then I could take the next train.
If we could be sure,
we'd let it go,
why defer to reason, restraint?'

For many nights,
I dream of her burial:
gravediggers consume vodka, eat sour bread

DEBORAH EMMANUEL

is a Singaporean poet, performer and professional speaker. She has performed her slam poetry at the Barcelona International Poetry Festival, Q Berlin Questions and TEDx Singapore, and has been invited as a resident to esteemed places like The Watermill Centre and Literarisches Colloquium Berlin. Deborah is the author of *When I Giggle in My Sleep* (2015), *Rebel Rites* (2016) and *Genesis Visual Poetry Collection* (2018). When not writing or performing poetry, she makes music with Mantravine, Wobology and Kiat, teaches workshops, paints/illustrates, devises independent theatre and travels to other dimensions.

SILENT REVOLUTION

In the spaces between these words,
first light blooms upon a mountain of
shadow.

All that is hidden floats to the surface,
dying fish rising out of the ocean.

All that was unsaid dangles in the air,
a delicate mobile dancing into form.

In solitude, resilience springs forth,
a fountain which did not know itself.

In the chasms between each sound
whole civilisations are found

birthing themselves   from the rubble,
peeling away bandages   from forgotten fruit,
striking matches   for a new fire.

A fragile world

crumbles   to become

a

perfect circle.

A star shines bright in a traffic-void sky.   From the silence,

a single breath
is drawn
into
the belly
of the universe,

releasing winds of revolution upon an unsuspecting earth.

THÉRÈSE FENSHAM

is a South African poet living in Cape Town. She completed her honours in journalism at the University of Stellenbosch in 1986. She has published a number of poems on Litnet. In 2018, her flash fiction piece was published in the literary magazine *Type/Cast*. She has also published poetry on AVBOB's poetry website.

LOSING YOU

On a day when that old moon was weary
and the city of my bones could only sigh,
you came to lift me.
Had I known you were only here on
borrowed time,
I would have built a moat, wide and deep
that no creature can defy,
and a dome not of wood, but pure granite
to coddle you.
I would have painted the sky a sinless coal,
no random worlds to touch or fray,
a mattress of fire to hold you,
and so much more, if only I could,
but would you have lived then?

TRAVELLER

Free spirit
far from the tree,
who made your hat
with its brim
so wide it caught
the Laptev sea?
Clothed your feet
in milled rags from
the wanton sewers
of Bangladesh?

Who fashioned
your dream coat

stitch by stitch
from tumultuous
Iowa straw you could
not
or would not ignore?
It must have taken
more than a year.

It did not stop
you from seeing
Kununurra
Kagga Kamma
Kaliningrad
it did not stop you
at
all.

Ribald notes
could not interfere
with the rousing
in you
and
yet
almost always
your bed was made.
Crimson berth it was,
locked you solid,
no one could leave.
There you had to lie.

But your very own
sweet reveries,
from
Babbitt
to Bogogoba,

that presumptuous
coil of living,
like bloodletting
to stem the throbbing,
can and will
in the final citation
never
ever
allow
itself
to
be
stymied.

JACK FOLEY

is an American poet living in Oakland, California. Foley's career as a poet is unique because it has always involved performance, specifically the presentation of 'multi-voiced' pieces written by Foley and performed by both Foley and his late wife.

AFTER NASHE

Darknesse falls from the air
All things deathe will snare
Lungs may burst and fayle
What is good turn stayle
Lips you wished to kiss
Soon will turn amiss
Marilyn Monroe
Into death did go
A burthen is the skye
I am sick, I must die.
Lord, have mercy on us

See the virus crowne
Burn our cities downe
Think of great New Yorke
All is devils worke
Men are shut and banned
Do not touch my hand
(Touch may mean your deathe)
Infected is the earthe
Infected is the skye
I am sick, I must die
Lord, have mercy on us.

EASTER 2020: THE MAN WHO DIED

another package of weird
toilet paper delivered—
can we find
dishwashing liquid

anywhere—
which Vietnamese
restaurant is open
today—
eggs are scarce
this Easter
—recollections of Syria
2003:
a lovely Muslim man
told me Muslims didn't believe
Jesus died on the cross,
which was why the tomb
was empty,
he went, perhaps, 'underground'
for a time

no bishops no kings
no resurrection no Christians
desire
is at the heart of it all
we move in the dark
as blind as the characters
in Saramago's novel
moving in a dark contagion
which is somehow 'white'—
what is 'blind
faith' if not desire
and what is resurrection
but the desire for life
asserting itself
even in the face of death
Which of us wants to die?
All faith is blind
We believe the flowers

that spring up from underground
promise us life
and that the man on the cross
whose body dies and comes back
says the same
and what if it isn't true
what if it isn't true?

—contagion takes us
Anyway

SARABJEET GARCHA

is a widely published bilingual poet from India. He is the author of four books of poems, including *A Clock in the Far Past*. He has translated several American poets into Hindi, including W.S. Merwin and John Haines, and several Indian poets into English, among them Mangalesh Dabral and Leeladhar Jagoori. He has also translated more than fifteen Marathi poets into both Hindi and English. The recipient of a fellowship from the Ministry of Culture of India, Sarabjeet is the founder and editorial director of Copper Coin, a multilingual publishing company.

THE GIRL OF FIFTEEN

(*for Jyoti Kumari*)

The heart her only guide, she spares
her body the desire to sprawl
under the neem tree back home.

The road her only prod, she dares
the tarmac vapours rising up
to become her noonday bandanna.

Her dad on pillion, she flares
her way into the darkness the sun
pistons into her head.

The girl of fifteen cycles
her injured father home.

She cycles into the wrecking ball
of heat that an unseen operator
swings full throttle towards her.

She cycles over the mirages
that megapolises raise on every path
those like her would ever walk.

She cycles into the man-size
LCD screens that never
tire of flashing lies.

She cycles into the light
caught in the pages
of *The Book of Miracles.*

The girl of fifteen cycles
her dream of home, home.

She writes with her feet the names
of all the dead migrants into the DNA
of roads that stretch to eternity.

She writes the names of the lame
who've pawned themselves in a game
only the chessmaster understands.

She writes the one rule
only a woman knows by birth:
In my house, nobody dies of hunger.

She writes *thunder*
on the skin of the sky drummed
by the tears of the abandoned.

Pumping the pedals
as if to crush Death himself,
the girl of fifteen cycles
the souls of the wounded home.

STOPOVER

Nanak in the ruins outside a village.
The word *come* is dearer to him
than *go*, so instead of *Go, Mardana,* he says
Come, Mardana. Make yourself at home.

The night a wordless companion,
they both take in cicada song,
a music much older than the walls
gnawed off by that beast known as time.

Give the rabab a rest, he hears Nanak say.
Mardana nestles the instrument into
what must have once been an alcove
for toy, bangle, turban and diya alike.

A fallen roofbeam for a pillow, the dirt floor
for a bed and the still air for a blanket

was much more than the pupil spurned
by a whole village could have asked for.

He tries, but can't take his eyes
off the cold mud stove in the corner.
His lips remember the taste of a river,
his hands the clasp of the master

who can let go of the whole world
but never of those who choose to rise.
His only wish tonight is to find
a ruse to forgive, a means to fill

his eyes with the sleep of the guru,
to see that which never sleeps,
his ears awake to the one voice
repeating, *Come, Mardana.*

Dream time's over. Arise.

AVRIL GARDINER

is a writer from Cape Town, South Africa. He is the curator of the Liebrecht Art Gallery in Somerset West, RSA. He has written seventy-seven sonnets in Afrikaans published as *Boeretroos* in 2018.

VEILS OR SAILS

(for Claude Debussy)

Hell hath no fire like a woman unveiled
Igniting a blaze behind the cloth of desire
A fever unmasked, a passion un-jailed
Embers rekindled behind the sensuous attire

And a candle once lit will not be derailed
A willing seller and willing buyer
A runaway fire will not be snailed
Exhausting the fuel of the willing supplier

But the law of combustion attraction requires
A fatal attraction conflagration obeys
A moth to a candle to fuel the desires
Foiling the mistress' moody malaise

The lesson in love will always prevail:
From fire to fury when the sailor sets sail

MAX GARLAND

is a well-known American poet whose most recent book, *The Word We Used for It*, won the Brittingham Poetry Prize. He received a fellowship from the National Endowment for the Arts, and his work has appeared in *Poetry, Gettysburg Review, Best American Short Stories* and many other journals and anthologies. Born in Kentucky, where he worked as a rural letter carrier on the route where he was born, he is professor emeritus at University of Wisconsin-Eau Claire, and the former Poet Laureate of Wisconsin.

SOCIAL DISTANCING

Say there came a pandemic; some news-drunk virus
set its hooks in us. And only the sky for a nurse,
arced and empty and barely even blue.

And only the musical pulse, and the several senses
for consolation, except for a stream of distant words
like waves bearing the rush, curl and foam of elsewhere

arriving, the distant rhythm of others to bridge the gap
between head and heart, dark and day, fear and whatever
it is one feels on the brink of

when walking next to great waters, how the surf catches
and releases the light, and the waves and bones tremble
like the distant cousins of constant thunder.

We know salt tumbles eventually from ocean to body
and back, and forth. We know it takes ages to regather
the shaken self into the good world again.

I remember a ritual once where hundreds of tiny
basket-like boats were lit and launched with prayers
and flowers and misfortunes, ignited and cast out

on the water until the bay was ablaze, a rocking
constellation of human woe uttered in small tongues
of flame, until little by little they drifted, burned,

blinked out, and then it was just dark water again,
and we all went home. Did our troubles never return?
Were we really less burdened, or better people?

What I mean is sometimes worry needs to be ignited,
launched into words, if only to blaze awhile among
flotillas of sorrows we thought were ours alone.

What I really mean, of course, is *Keep in touch.*
Even if you don't know what to say, *especially*
if you don't know what to say. *Kind words,*

fellow castaways, mind-lit emergencies of fingertip
and tongue, float this festival of downtime and distance,
repopulate the dark with your fledgling human light.

NORBERT GORA

is a Polish poet. He is the author of three books of poetry, *Globe Bathed in Horror*, *Darkness in the End* and *There Must be Something between Dark and Light*. His work has appeared in several journals and anthologies published in many countries. He is attracted to speculative fiction and emotional poetry. He deals mostly with death, suffering and mystery.

THE REAL VIRUS

The sky is as clear
as the surface of the lake,
when people are locked
up in their homes,
an unexpected thought
entered the mind horizons,
who exactly
is the virus here?

SEEDS OF DISTRUST

The distance must be kept,
contactless community,
closeness like a forbidden thing
has been already banned.

Day by day
seeds of distrust grow,
they came to fertile ground
and finally they will cover
homes, streets, entire cities,
no one will look
beyond suspicion,
trailer from life
after the pestilence.

AMLANJYOTI GOSWAMI

grew up in Guwahati and lives in New Delhi. He has been published in journals and anthologies around the world. His recent collection, *River Wedding* (Poetrywala), has been widely reviewed. His poems have also appeared on street walls of Christchurch, exhibitions in Johannesburg, an e-gallery in Brighton and buses in Philadelphia. He has read in various places, including in New York, New Delhi and Boston.

IN TIME

In time, all this will be distant
As last night's faded dream.

Our eyes will flicker at the word
Our hearts will miss a beat

When we remember these days,
How an ambulance at the door spelt danger, not hope.

How we looked away from each other
With a measured distance, perfect strangers living together.

In time, we will be more at home
With our many imperfections, our perfect solitude.

We will know how to divide our sorrows, multiply joys,
Like a method actor with many parts, each part a life.

In time, we will learn to eat, a morsel in our palms,
We will learn the meaning of taste.

And what it is to have enough.
We will be sometimes reborn of solitude

That finds us finally whole
After all those years of searching.

In time. All in good time.
The poet will find the words to live

And this will become novel
As a hatchback turtle cab

Crawling the foggy streets of New York, or Kolkata
In the yellow light, hard to tell car from colour.

In time, we will even forget faces
Those in white, warriors wielding scalpels who tunnelled
through

And we will forget to thank them, we will forget
Their names, what they ate, what it felt to be around them

Their common destinies, their life stories.
Their hopes, their little fears, their moments of joy.

We will look back one day, and wonder
What drove us, fear or hope,

The gulp in our throats or survival written in our code.
The fear in our lips, or the joy of our songs.

What drew us together even as we grew apart.
Our friendship in hardship.

In time, we might remember to call each other home
Like the old days, when growing up meant strangers in our
    midst.

We may even find the meaning of time
When we go out and meet the sun, at our pace.

When night falls, past midnight, we will haunt that old bar
Where the barman with half a smoke and broken eyes

Plays those blues from the old days
And says he prefers poetry to the sound of silence.

We will remember him, even as he no longer remembers us.
And we will think of hope, its absence of thought, its perfect
    belief.

When generations on, ask us, what it was like,
We will tell them, yes, we kissed with our eyes,

Learnt how to live, a day at a time, not a breath too soon,
How we never found the time to die.

DIARY

He kept a diary, of walking movements
Inside the house.
It recorded every step in detail.
He was troubled over the basics
Which foot would go in first,
Why did the ground hold firm this time?
What made the air move?

But what perplexed him
(Yes, he read in secret)
Was the Pythagoras triangle
He seemed to follow—
Two ends of the pyramid
Dining table to bedroom door
Towards a point that ended in shadow.

A right angle that wasn't quite
In step. A little out of line.
He measured his weariness
To a fine perfection, of broken points
Stop start stops, jumping over the line
As if he were playing (with himself)
Tic tac toe.

HILDEBRANDO PEREZ GRANDES

is a Peruvian poet living in Lima. He follows the poetic principles of the 1960s modernists like Javier Heraud and Antonio Cisneros. His poems have been translated into English, French, German and Portuguese. He has been a regular and visiting professor in universities and director of La Revista de Poesia Pielago.

HOWLING*

Introduce me into your arteries, what else
I would like to, be your blood
Your delirium. Your favourite song.
Light up the river
Of tigers
Derailed
They knock us out. Already
I don't know if it's the ambulance
The one that goes through
The deserted streets
To help someone,
To someone
Or am I the one, dying,
Moriamando, to die loving.
Those who are about to die,
Call for help, help, help
Tonight
That you will never forget. The truth
I just keep on howling,
Auuuuuuuuu
Auuuuuuuuuuuu
And the ambulance
Like you, without mercy, he ignores me.

**Translated from the Spanish by Nishi Chawla.*

ZOOM*

How I would like to bite your ears, your lilies
That escape my zoom and
From the desk
Already charred by my love
No mask, no gel
No health notices.
How much would I give to devour you,
No alarms, anxieties,
Fears, prophecies and viruses,
That erase your syllables,
Your mud and your chemistry
They are already trembling
Turning off your image, ay, turning off,
My zoom, my animal, my geography.

*Translated from the Spanish by Nishi Chawla.

JOY HARJO

is the author of nine poetry collections, including the national bestseller *An American Sunrise*, and a memoir, *Crazy Brave*. A member of the Muscogee (Creek) Nation, Harjo was named US Poet Laureate in 2019. She lives in Tulsa, Oklahoma.

I GIVE YOU BACK

I release you, my beautiful and terrible
fear. I release you. You were my beloved
and hated twin, but now, I don't know you
as myself. I release you with all the
pain I would know at the death of
my children.

You are not my blood anymore.

I give you back to the soldiers
who burned down my house, beheaded my children,
raped and sodomized my brothers and sisters.
I give you back to those who stole the
food from our plates when we were starving.

I release you, fear, because you hold
these scenes in front of me and I was born
with eyes that can never close.

I release you
I release you
I release you
I release you

I am not afraid to be angry.
I am not afraid to rejoice.
I am not afraid to be black.
I am not afraid to be white.
I am not afraid to be hungry.
I am not afraid to be full.
I am not afraid to be hated.
I am not afraid to be loved.

to be loved, to be loved, fear.

Oh, you have choked me, but I gave you the leash.
You have gutted me but I gave you the knife.
You have devoured me, but I laid myself across the fire.

I take myself back, fear.
You are not my shadow any longer.
I won't hold you in my hands.
You can't live in my eyes, my ears, my voice
my belly, or in my heart my heart
my heart my heart

But come here, fear
I am alive and you are so afraid
of dying.

KARABI DEKA HAZARIKA

is an Assamese poet and academician. She has taught as a professor of Comparative Indian Literature and was dean at Dibrugarh University in Assam, India. She has also authored several books for children.

THE LOCKDOWN DIARY

The morning sun that crept in
clutched on the whole day
Just refusing to go away.
Light today has the most critical of tasks,
shining over a hidden page tucked, folded amidst old clothes
a dried petal of white rose
forgotten inside some timeless pages
those words written, overwritten
time and again
across the old diary pages,
gloating over all these,
with a smile the sunlight asks—
well then? What is it all about?
Sucharita pretended not to hear.
Throughout the old pages
in the middle of arranging the house
Her fingers are on a constant search
For the essence of it all,
of a life routinized.
Like a spotted butterfly trapped in the spiderweb,
that river,
that rain,
those nights,
Like beings unshakable,
are crawling out of the pages
and pulling at the folds of her 'rehaa'
Beyond the green curtain lies a limitless sky
The one inside is tiny
but intimate, with far more intense shades of blue
The lights caressed her face softly and whispered—
but this is time to talk to oneself

to seek yourself in the sky
to look for your face in the water
to set your little boat of tears and joy on a sail.
Holding the flowers made of light in both her hands
as golden as the mustard fields
that lit up one's teen and youth

Sucharita dips into
the golden
content and blissful
like a pigeon in her happy nest.
She spreads the happiness in little quantities
across the tiny beaks around
in this home shaded by clouds,
sleep comes floating as a regal experience.
The sun spoke up, all of a sudden:
Stay well, Sucharita,
the hours of darkness are the ones most luminous.
At the end of tonight
will come
The golden lit dawn.
This,
in the scale of life's entirety,
is your very own time, Sucharita,
your very own time.
The sun goes down.
In that scant forest
sprung up across the room locked down
Sucharita's entire life
stays afloat
as a sparkling firefly.

GEOFFREY HIMES

is an American music critic and poet. His poetry has been published by *December*, *Delaware Poetry Review*, *Salt Lick*, *Baltimore City Paper* and other publications. His song lyrics have been set to music by Si Kahn, Walter Egan, Pete Kennedy, Billy Kemp, Fred Koller and others.

MARCH 2020

The weather outside is springlorious,
sun-soaked, green-grassed, daffodil-dappled.
It's the weather inside, within our bodies,
that is storm-blown and ice-locked.
Tiny, spiky balls bounce through our arteries,
pinballs no flippers can stop
from the cavities they crave.
They drop into our lungs, where they
hatch babies like rabbits in skin-shiny lesions.

Whenever we open the front door,
We're masked like outlaws, gloved like butlers.
The only thing we can share is distance,
measured by the length of a corpse.
When we walk through petal-twirling breezes,
sharp knives, too small to see,
seeking our orifices, come flying.

After many months of purgatory,
when the now blossom-blanketed trees
are bare and dusted with snow,
what will we salvage from the wreckage?
When the windscape turns wintry,
will our insides at long last have their
springlorious breaking of buds into blossoms?

PERFORMING ARTS CENTRES

If I read one more simpering poem,
full of flowers and abstract nouns,

or hear one more sensitive song,
full of arpeggios and winding paths,
I swear I'm going to burn down
a performing arts centre.

Don't you get it? Nature isn't going to save us.
The coronavirus is nature.
That microscopic ball with the hooks
is an organism as committed to its own survival
and as indifferent to ours
as the shadiest apple tree in bloom.

Nature is as terrifying as it is inspiring,
and anyone who doesn't acknowledge
both halves of that truth
disrespects nature as much as the worst polluter.
Bambi is nature, but so is the fire
that killed her mother.

But nature is all we've got,
from the smallest virus to the proudest ape.
No puppetmaster is dangling the marionette strings
No ghosts are pushing around the furniture.
The virus wants the wet warmth of our lungs,
and so do we. Who will be the smarter?

I'm not really going to burn down
a performing arts centre,
but I am going to picture it in my mind:
those not-so-smart sensitive souls screaming,
their rose-tinted glasses cracking in the heat,
their peasant-chic shirts smoking on their backs.

SOCIAL DISTANCE

We'd been dating for a few weeks
When the coronavirus came.
I thought that we'd grow closer,
But things remained the same.

She said I shouldn't touch her.
She said I should wash my hands,
Dry them off and stick them both
In the pockets of my pants.

Should we keep a social distance,
Maybe six feet, maybe more?
She said we should, although we had
Never been that close before.

She said we shouldn't kiss or hug,
Or sit close knee-to-knee,
Was she avoiding the virus,
Or was she avoiding me?

'To protect the population,'
She said, 'Let's stay in after dark.
We should stay away from movies,
Nightclubs, restaurants and parks.'

She said, 'No, don't sit too close;
You're better off over there.
Don't you know that micro-spores
Are floating in the air?'

Should we keep a social distance,
Maybe six feet, maybe more?
She said we should, although we had
Never been that close before.

She said we shouldn't kiss or hug,
Or sit close knee-to-knee,
Was she avoiding the virus,
Or was she avoiding me?

'In fact,' she said, 'we're better off
If we both stay home alone.
You can call me now and then,
But first sanitize your phone.'

This evening after dinner,
I saw her walking hand-in-hand
With a richer, taller, handsome guy
And I began to understand.

Should we keep a social distance,
Maybe six feet, maybe more?
She said we should, although we had
Never been that close before.

She said we shouldn't kiss or hug,
Or sit close knee-to-knee,
Was she avoiding the virus,
Or was she avoiding me?

SIBUSISO HLATSHWAYO

(stage name *blessedm*) hails from the far east of Ekurhuleni in Brakpan (Tsakane), South Africa. He started writing in 1999 and studied music between 2003 and 2006, playing the piano. In 2007 and 2008, he studied music production with Soul Candi Institute of Music. He has been a student at Mzansi Poetry Academy and is a co-founder of a writer's organization called Imbuyezi and the African Revolution Community Development.

TWO MINIMS

Listen to your surroundings
you shall hear a jazz piece,

If there is no music in your ears
Then you have not turned in,
You have missed the frequency.
What time did you arrive at the station?

A 3/8 or a 6/8 are my only time signatures.
A 4/4 is out of the question.
My life is not worth two minims

Emasimini the wind
blows through the dry crops.
Forming the sqUicky saW thRoat SoUnds of the saXophone.

Two semitones down the chromatic scale of life,
the birds were born to sing.
But you were born singing,
Those who witnessed your birth just called it crying.

Listen to your surroundings
you shall hear a jazz piece titled *Mandulo*.
My life is not worth two minims.

WHEN A TRUMPETER DIES

My fingers become mouthpieces
When I play the piano, the singer depends on me
I cannot allow the trio to be a duet

When a trumpeter dies
his breath remains
To blow the talk of time
For centuries to come

When a trumpeter dies
His life of works ascends to a place in the mind
called remembrance. Give me a swing
Was the trumpeter's last request.

RANJIT HOSKOTE

is a poet, cultural theorist and curator from India. He is the author of seven books of poetry, including, most recently, *Central Time* (Penguin/Viking, 2014), *Jonahwhale* (Penguin/Hamish Hamilton, 2018) and *The Atlas of Lost Beliefs* (Arc, 2020). His translation of a fourteenth-century Kashmiri woman mystic's work has appeared as *I, Lalla: The Poems of Lal Ded* (Penguin Classics, 2011). He is the editor of *Dom Moraes: Selected Poems* (Penguin Modern Classics, 2012). Hoskote has been honoured with the Sahitya Akademi Golden Jubilee Award, the Sahitya Akademi Translation Award, and the S.H. Raza Award for Literature. His poems have been translated into German, Hindi, Marathi, Gaelic, Swedish, Spanish and Arabic.

AUBADE

Rumours of wind, banners of cloud.
The low earth shakes but the storm
has not arrived. You pack

for the journey, look up, look through
the doors at trees shedding their leaves
too soon, a track on which silk shoes
would be wasted, a moon

still dangling above a boat.
Wearing your salt mask, you face
the mulberry shadows.
The valley into which
you're rappelling

is you.

RETREAT

This floor is wet with the sea's retreat
                    A draggled wing
drapes its shadow on the bell tower

Admiral, your telescope!
                                        Hold fast
The storm could have knuckled you to the floor

Voices wash through the sailor's sleep
          He scoops darkness
from darkness

The surveyor continues to look
                    for a world at the other end
of his spyglass

knowing it's out there

a distant cousin to the one

that's blowing up around him

BREATH

If that was breath I saw floating across the tracks
without a single train to stop it
while the parrots squawked in their fruited tree
I knew it would far outdistance the night

spelling itself in one language after another along the route

leaving me to catch up
halting and ranging in its wake
calling out to it by every name
I have waited all my life to speak

BED

A bed used to stand
in that room of shimmering tides
Now a boat

rides at anchor there
caulked
and ready to sail

through the mother-of-pearl shutters
We are
what we've lost

BABITHA MARINA JUSTIN

is a poet, an artist and an academic. Her poems and short stories have appeared in many national and international journals. Her published collections of poems are *Of Fireflies, Guns and the Hills* and *I Cook My Own Feast*.

WRITING FROM MY NEIGHBOURHOOD

Homes are silent:
children no longer play
in the bylanes, picking up
flying frisbees, burying butterflies,
I can smell chickpeas
sautéed in garam masala
from my neighbour's kitchen.
Her quiet daughters have
become quieter.

My mongrel is the one
who has no panic button on.

He sleeps dreaming of his bitch:
she hovers around
my house, sniffing (every corner
where he had pissed) and whining
in love, he darts to the gate,
they sniff-kiss each other, like refugees
from two warring countries:
Home and Street.

When once my mother
was returning home,
the bitch hid her tail between her legs
slunk in the street-corner with a whine
like the docile daughter-in-law
in the sitcoms that everybody
watches sitting at home
during Corona times.

My father, at seventy-five,
sits in a corner,

watching sports highlights,
reading the news on TV
throughout the tone-deaf day,
at times he takes a glimpse
at YouTube videos of
sniff-kissing love
in the time of quarantine.

My boys make hay out of
this quarantine, they mouth it
like a lollipop, they're socially distant
preferring online games to playgrounds,
malls to seashores,
they build tents out of
their own bubbles.

I have to go out and smell
the sea and feel its filthy frothy
gums sucking on my toes,

I want to break the roof,
let lovelorn leaves fall on my
bed, I want to stretch
on the ground branching out
my tendrils with the roots.

I have travelled a long way
from my neighbourhood.

MANGESH NARAYANRAO KALE

is a poet, painter, editor and art critic. He is the author of five major books of poems in Marathi, including *Mayaviye Tahrir* (Writing is Bewitching), and two books of art criticism. He has won multiple awards for his outstanding contribution to Marathi literature, including the Maharashtra Foundation Award (USA), Bhavabhuti Award, and Yashwantrao Chavan Award. He has also received three fellowships, including one from the India Foundation for the Arts. Kale is the founding editor of *Khel*, an acclaimed little magazine that has published several special issues celebrating the works of the finest poets writing in Marathi, including Vasant Abaji Dahake, Dilip Chitre, Vasant Dattatreya Gurjar, Tulsi Parab, Raja Dhale and Vilas Sarang, among others. His artworks have been exhibited all over India and abroad in both solo and group shows, and his essays on art and literature are regularly published in the most widely circulated periodicals of Maharashtra. He lives and works in Pune.

ALL ALONE*

He stays alone in the house
his wife and children occupy the same house
even then he is all alone in the house

the wife has a house within the house
she stays alone in that house
and he too is all alone in the house

the children too have a house within the house
they stay alone in that house
even then he is all alone in his house

loneliness has a house within the house
loneliness also stays alone in that house
even then he is all alone in the house

a house within the house also stays alone
a house absolutely has a house
and he is all alone in the house at night

he stays alone in the house
his wife and son and daughter also stay alone
even loneliness stays all alone in the house

he stays alone in the house

---

* *Translated from the Marathi by Sarabjeet Garcha.*

DEAL*

He heaved his shadow
over his shoulder
and started walking

his shadow heaved him
over its shoulder
and started walking

the deal between the two
is to keep talking
Whoever stops
will have his head smashed
into a thousand pieces

hanging the shadow on a tree
he can walk out of the situation
even then the talking won't stop

heaving the shadow over its shoulder
the tree will start walking
or the tree's shadow
will heave the tree over its shoulder

the deal between the two
is to keep walking
Whoever stops
will have its head smashed
into a thousand pieces

possibly the tree will stop
after entrusting the shadow to the wind
even then the sequence won't change
The shadow on its shoulder

** Translated from the Marathi by Sarabjeet Garcha.*

the wind will keep rushing
or the wind on its shoulder
the shadow of the wind will keep rushing
constantly

the deal between the two
is to keep rushing
Whoever stops
will have its head smashed
into a thousand pieces

JOANNA KANIA

is a Polish poet. She lives in Poland where she teaches English as a second language. She also runs two blogs.

REMEMBERING

While COVID-19 was on its world tour 2020
it wasn't to win an entrance to all the stages,
some stages were reserved
for other occurrences

like a cat's quiet dying
on Good Friday—a day
as good as any other one
to die—and for the simple reason
that
'one's time has come'. All her life
she lived
in our garden, half-wild and half-
domesticated. Light brown, like soil.

We called her *mother.*
One would assume she hadn't deserved
a proper name. But all we meant
was to honour her sacred role
of giving birth. Far from
the shiniest and the most robust,
she gave the world
four litters
of kittens. The first one

was just one black *little devil*—he was
the sweetest thing in our backyard.
Then three black kittens
two of whom did not live through
the summer. And then, again,
two cutest blackies
born at the start
of May the year that followed.

The last time she had kittens,
she had five (one that survived
the eye plague
that usually proves fatal
among little cats). We found
a family for each one of them

for they were small
and the fall was coming.

The *mother* had her pleasures, too:
her birthright share of hay and sunshine,
the shade of trees, the green
of grass, the food, the shelter
of a wooden shack. It's there

where she gave out
her last sigh. We found her lying
on Father's weathered coat
near the basket where she sometimes slept.
In fact, she looked not dead
but sleeping. Mother

took her out and wrapped her
in a soft white cloth, and Father

took her to the nearby wood
where he buried her under
a gathering of trees. He said
the dirt was soft
and loving

and in the leaves
there was
a humming sound
to watch over
her

ANGSHUMAN KAR

is a Bengali poet and novelist. He is a professor of English at the University of Burdwan, West Bengal, India. He was also secretary of Sahitya Akademi, Eastern Region, and member of its advisory board (Bengali). He has fourteen collections of poems, four novels, three novellas, a collection of short stories and two memoirs to his credit. Kar has received seven awards, including the Krittibas Puroskar, Bangiyo Sahityo Parishad Puroskar and the Paschim Banga Bangla Akademi Puroskar.

NOT A DREAM*

The arrow kept in the quiver
has not venom but love on its head.
After emerging from the rocket launcher
What crosses the border
is hydroxychloroquine.
What you consider
an armour
is actually a PPE.
And instead of shields
the soldiers are carrying
either sanitizers or soaps.

For the first time
The world is witnessing a horrific war
without weapons!

Translated from the Bengali by the poet.

ANJUM
KATYAL

is a writer, editor and translator. She has been chief editor of Seagull Books as well as editor of *Seagull Theatre Quarterly*. She is the author of several books on theatre, including *Habib Tanvir: Towards an Inclusive Theatre* and *Badal Sircar: Towards a Theatre of Conscience*. She has also translated plays by Habib Tanvir, Usha Ganguli's *Rudali* and stories by Mahasweta Devi and Meera Mukherjee. She is a published poet. She has been director, Apeejay Kolkata Literary Festival, and curator, Nabanna Earth Weekend (NEW) festival of arts and ideas. She also sings the blues.

SEPARATION

Time stirs its sluggish spoon.

Blocks of stolid day hours
shift. Angle. Wheel. Turn.
Military manoeuvres
in perfect step.

But as day softens into sleep
thickening the flesh of trees,
slabs of a rich, buttery light
I long to share with you.

ROAMING

The miracle of space that is the mind.
Memory, the heart's treasure chest.
With its rooms, courtyards, gardens, streets.
Cities, valleys, banks and shores.
The same street over decades.
The same room over a lifetime.
We visit, we linger, we return . . .

And we are warmed once more
by the sunlight slanting in through that window,
stirred by the shadows resting in those corners,
cooled by that stone floor under our feet.
The curve of a road.
The swell of a wave breaking jade
fragile on the sand.
The heat of a rock we rest against.

The intimate geographies of desire.
The infinite geography of the mind.

WAQAS KHWAJA

is a Pakistani poet and writer teaching in the US. He is the Ellen Douglass Leyburn Professor of English at Agnes Scott College, Atlanta, Georgia, where he teaches postcolonial literature, eighteenth- and nineteenth-century British literature, and creative writing. He has published four collections of poetry, a literary travelogue about his experiences with the International Writing Program at the University of Iowa, and several edited anthologies of Pakistani literature in translation.

ON THE SECOND DAY

On the second day I had it all worked out,
Except I was not yet able to distinguish darkness from light
When I stepped into the backyard,
Stirring already with commotion—
No serpent to tempt me, though there once was
A garter snake with three yellow stripes along its body
Trapped in the net spread over the pond to protect the fish
From the vast-winged great blue heron of the East
Who had taken a liking to dining on such easy prey,
But it had been carefully untangled and released
To slide away to its refuge in some shady part
Of the garden and hadn't shown itself since—
All fuss and flurry at this hour, the unlocking
Of tiny shuttered nodes and nubs to let shoots through,
And young stalks, and germinating leaves,
Their tongues gingerly stretched to sip on fresh breeze,
While a pair of doves flew down from somewhere
Picking in fern and grass by the waterfall,
And, before long, a thrasher and its mate joined them,
Floating to the wet stone steps, their feet in tumbling water,
Their heads bobbing under it, flittering and fluttering their
wings—
Now a bluebird comes looking for its mealworms,
A spangle of hummingbirds blazes at the feeder,
And those overgrown, greedy squirrels scurry about,
Sit back on their haunches and nibble away
At all they can find, never satisfied, making sure
They get the best pick before any others arrive,
Crested cardinals, in pairs, the strutting, flaunting-red male
And the steady, olive-bronze, fire-tinged female,
And here come the rest of the regulars,

Wrens, robins, mocking birds, goldfinches,
Chickadees, house sparrows, even a blue jay,
Suddenly agitating trees humming quietly in their vernal
    leaves,
To raise a chorus of calls, titters and chirps, whistles, coos,
    and trills,
Flying down in ones and twos to check out
Loose hung baskets and plates stocked with birdfeed—
There now, a couple of cottontails, hop lightly into view,
Sniffing in the vegetable patch, looking suspiciously around,
Their nostrils flare and flicker, their eyes
Alert to the sparrow hawk high up in the maple—
And imperceptibly even as attention is absorbed
By all that is stirring and happening all around
Light breaks free of darkness and brushes first the tops of trees,
An extravagant display of greens in a wash of liquid gold,
Stippled with pinks and splotched with crimsons,
Strokes down their smooth or chequered trunks
And sweeps clean across the lawn as it flows
To the street below, quiet and deserted at this hour,
Its sombre grey fringing the landscaped view—
Nobody would know we are in a lockdown here,
She and I, just the two of us, together, from as long
As it seems the beginning of all time, the end of it,
Or that a phantom sovereign gone viral
Continues to reproduce itself
Not only in what we witness within and around us,
But in forms and colours we may not know,
Cannot yet imagine, see or have not the capacity to see,
Quite another life, another world, active, dynamic, secreted
Beyond the eye and ear, the nose, the tongue, the fingertip,
Teeming, prowling, seeking to escape its corrals and cages,
Spill out into the world we perceive, undo and disassemble it,

Take away its forms, its dies and tints, its proportions and scale,
Strangely, precariously, held together against this impulse
To shatter entirely its already permeable walls and screens.

II

The world, its shapes and shades, its cares crowd in—
The school bus arrives on the street below,
Not to pick up kids for school
But to deliver their breakfast—it will return again
In the afternoon with lunch, even here, in this neighbourhood,
A reminder it won't be the second day forever—
Nor is it now, for already weeks, or perhaps eons have passed,
And the world, dreamt into existence and inhabited,
There's little else to do, except to watch it spiral
On its fine-tuned course to its inevitable destination—
Of all that is planned, and what indeed is embedded within
To disrupt or defeat it.
Back in our house of confinement
The ordinary plays itself out with unerring fidelity—
Late mornings, unsettled by a headache, news,
The chastening toll of infections and deaths over breakfast,
Virtual peddling of learning and skills, not much rated in the
best of times,
To others equally dubious, equally dispirited and dismayed,
Anxieties more exacting with each passing day,
Long evening strolls on half-deserted streets,
Weekly excursions for provisions,
Uneasy with others about for the same purpose,
Striding by with the same alarm—
In all this commonplace newness,
The urge to write poems that will not be coaxed,
Cannot be enticed, unless they come in defiance,
Resist and revoke all that you thought about art and life—
Simple clichés of our ho-hum lives that survive all catastrophes:

Neither happiness nor sorrow comes unmingled with its opposite,
Our world is prey perpetually to contradictions,
This too will go away, things will change, there's light ahead—
And the everyday takes over the uncommon,
Savings sink, endowments plummet,
And individuals and institutions that depend on them stagger
under the blow,
Trades and businesses crumble, jobs are extinguished,
And it is far more fatal for families without food,
Without means to maintain shelter over their heads,
For people friendless and forsaken, a bristling silence,
For the elderly and ailing, their shit and grime,
While nurses and physicians front the enemy in its lair,
And lab researchers seek to demystify its perplexing disposition—
Migrant labour on farms, in slaughterhouses and meat-packing
plants,
Drivers, grocery-store workers, warehouse packers, carriers,
Recalling attention to 'essential work' and 'essential workers',
Regularly disparaged, now regularly in demand,
Plucked even from loss-of-employment indemnification,
Regularly obliged to put themselves in danger,
For their disparagers as much as those indifferent to
Or unaware of their existence,
To ensure that supply of daily needs and services,
And profits, no doubt, is not interrupted—
'It is the economy, stupid!
The centre and the circumference of the universe,
The force that rules the planets and constellations,
The apple and the seeds at its core.
Time to reopen the marketplace of exchange and extraction,
No matter the risk. People die anyway.'—
Who does though, at the borders of peril and menace,
But the essentially expendable?

Those who gather profits, indulge their whims and
investments,
Are not the same who do the work to produce that wealth,
To enable that indulgence,
Their stakes and shares not the same—Clichés,
Our ordinary world, our ordinary lives are made up of them.
These are still the early days.

III

But birds and bees don't much concern themselves with this,
Trees rustle with delight in the breeze, insects go about as usual,
Fish in the pond chase each other with the abandon of the
breeding season,
And thick-skinned frogs imitate the sheep's bleating as
carelessly as ever,
Though the family of deer I saw one night under the cypresses,
That flicked their ears as I approached and sprinted away
through the lawn,
Is no more—the stag I saw two months ago, dead on the side of
the road
That leads to the highway, while the doe was hit by a speeding
truck
On a two-way city street less than a mile from our home, I
found out driving
Back from work one evening—only the fawn remains, a little
bigger now,
Magnificent though, as he grows into adulthood, but seen always
Wandering alone in the woods and cleared spaces
Between houses lining that city street where his mother was
killed—
What of that? Birds have declined by almost five billion these
last fifty years,
But you will not see any carcasses of birds anywhere!
And where are the swarms of butterflies?

The buzzing clouds of pollinating bees?
Underground, the red ants march in vast armies north across
the continent,
We make our own deserts and pretend they are fruit-bearing
orchards,
Hard cash, their fruit—Our enterprise wipes out
Millions of acres of earth's forests around the planet,
But we still have these, oak and hickory, tulip magnolia and
maple,
Beech and Leyland cypress, Yaupin holly and weeping red
dragon,
Chinese witch hazel, river birch, tea-olive, crepe myrtle,
All these cultivated varieties in our backyard, it is easy to forget
What is lost elsewhere, what ecological systems and micro-
ecologies,
Communities and life-forms native to territory and
environment—
So too, the population of rivers and seas,
Unsparingly harvested for what we did not sow,
To serve our tables and salons, pharmacies and ateliers,
Their fish and plant life, organisms that sustain them,
Their rich habitats, coral reefs, salt marshes, mangrove forests,
Expunged from the geological register—
There is no end in sight to our plundering for dividends—
Meanwhile, in our garden that has no gates, nor flaming
swords,
We mourn Xena, our turquoise-eyed, Siamese Tabby,
Who died last year after a warm companionship that lasted
eighteen years,
And quietly sleeps now under the ice-blue cypress in a grove
of trees
And shrubs beside the grass, lavender and rosemary growing at
her feet.

IV

So, truly, nothing is quite worked out,
Days and nights could just as well be nights and days,
I wouldn't care, it wouldn't matter—
But the brain-shattering white noise
That keeps minds and bodies chained
To the endless task of serving in anguish and despair,
Or just the sliver of a mirrored hope
That keeps them shackled to the daily grind,
Is broken, if only for a fragmentary slip in time,
And in this interval, in this very garden in the backyard,
Where no one is an intruder, no one under surveillance,
Where no whispering slanderer traduces or defames anyone,
Where no interdict or ban curtails the comings and goings,
No transgression, no judgment, no penalty, no retribution,
Right here, where exiled, we were meant to earn our keep,
With the bloodstained sweat of our humiliated brow,
May lie our only salvation, the redemption of reciprocal
exchange,
Of incessant transition and burgeoning that goes on all
around us,
From which we keep ourselves stubbornly in ravening
isolation.

MIKLAVŽ KOMELJ

is a Slovenian poet and art historian. He has published twelve books of poetry, two books of prose, a scientific monography about the Yugoslavian partisan art, a collection of essays about poetry, and several books and scientific articles and essays about the theory and history of art and literature. He is the recipient of numerous awards, including the Prešeren Foundation Prize, Jenko Prize, Veronika Prize and Igor Zabel working grant. He lives and works in Ljubljana as a freelancer writer.

FIFTEEN VOLCANOES

Fifteen volcanoes vomited
in the same night.

When the whole world is dominated by the forces
which no one
can dominate,
it is even more clear to me
that the whole world is a magical game
of my forces,
of your forces.

The flower of the aloe
invited a hummingbird,
that he came
to the flower of the aloe.
This hummingbird
which came
to the flower of the aloe,
invited the flower of the aloe,
that it rose
from the aloe.

Fifteen volcanoes vomited
in the same night.

And that gave a fearful purity
to the vomiting of the multitude.

They are trying
to get dirty,
that they would not need to live
with that fearful purity.
Yet no,
it is impossible to get dirty.

Even in the putrefying, there is the fearful purity
of the white bones;
the dancer doesn't connect them
with death,
for the dance is beyond
all the ties.

Fifteen volcanoes vomited
in the same night.

These are not ties.
The ties disguise
the meeting beyond
all the ties.
There is no excuse. It *is* my will.
It *is* your will.

Fifteen volcanoes vomited
in the same night!

ASHWANI KUMAR

is an Indian poet, writer, and professor at Tata Institute of Social Sciences, India. His latest collection of poems, *Banaras and the Other*, was longlisted for the Jayadev National Poetry Award. A collection of his poems, *Architecture of Alphabets*, has been published in Hungarian. He is also co-founder of Indian Novels Collective for translation of classic novels from Indian languages. He writes regularly for the *Financial Express*.

UNANNOUNCED COMMUNISM

After a long day's idleness—
No smell of burning pig iron or
Chimes of manufacturing happiness
My proletarian body parts
Barely moving
Rot, rust in the cold silence.
Your ash-green eyes are filled
With crumbs of falling stars
And I feel like a factory
Shutdown into unannounced communism.

FLAMINGOS IN EARLY SUMMER

Nobody thought
In the terrible days of solitude,
Herds of jobless migrants with clay brick masks would
Suddenly arrive in the lockdown city.

With them, the Armenian flamingos
Also descended; flock after flock
In the maggoty shadows of early summer.

From their sweaty pink wings,
Dry mustard leaves kept falling
In the freshly made shelter homes.

Flapping their empty stomachs,
Slowly, they filled the sky
With their hungry nasal cries for food and water.

Infuriated with the smell of infectious blood
Affluent city dwellers turned against themselves—
Speaking with strange voices of stones
In their moments of self-survival.

NILIM KUMAR

is the author of seventeen volumes of poetry and three novels in Assamese. His poetry has been translated into several languages, including English, French, Hindi, Marathi, Gujarati, Punjabi and Nepali. His poetry has won various accolades, including the Uday Bharati National Award, the Raza Foundation Award and the Shabda Award. He has participated in a number of national and international literary festivals.

IN LOVE WITH THE CORONA INFECTED*

1

As she returned from Italy,
she was already gasping for breath.

Those two hands that taught
mathematics to the students in Italy,

those two hands that I had
grabbed the moment we met,

those two hands that we had forgotten
whom they belonged to since we met—

those two hands today refused to touch
me; even my two hands were fearful.

Both our lips acted as if we hadn't
seen the quivering of each other's lips.

She beckoned me to the shores
of the Arabian Sea. She always said

she carried the waves of the sea
in her heartbeats, she always

started conversations of love
with these waves in her heart.

I said we'd sit at the distance of one metre.
She said one-and-a-half metres.

Always one-and-a-half metres, she insisted.
It's good to do math; she was good at math.

We did not utter a word. Our eyes spoke
everything that we wanted to share.

**Translated from the Assamese by Dibyajyoti Sarma.*

Seeing the flowing rivers of our eyes,
even the Arabian Sea was mournful.

She said, I have come to see you for
one last time. I informed the cops.

2

She was taken to a hospital, where
only the Covid-19 viruses spoke—

their conversations were sums of death
hurriedly jotted down with both hands.

She counted her heartbeats, our kisses,
our furtive touches and our sleeplessness.

She talked to the oxygen tank,
she called it with my name.

She knew how desperately I wanted
to be that oxygen tank for her.

3

Full of smiles one day
she descended the hospital stairs.

Looking at my moist eyes,
she asked, is the sea still there?

I said, you are my sea,
my heartbeats the waves.

Then we both raced
towards the seashore.

On her heart there was no fear,
on her heart was the sea's laughter.

Waiting to be wiped away by
our joy, the sands still bore

the footprints of police boots and
the one-and-a-half metre signs.

In that moment of touch,
in the unbroken embrace

we noticed on both our hearts
the rise and fall of the same waves—

the rise and fall of the same waves,
and their refusal to return.

MARRA PL. LANOT

is a Filipino poet, essayist and a freelance journalist who writes in Filipino, English and Spanish. She has published several books, including five collections of poetry, three collections of profiles and a book of essays, in addition to writing several teleplays. She has also taught literature, creative writing and film studies at the University of the Philippines, her alma mater. She is the recipient of the Gawad Balagtas 2020 for lifetime achievement in poetry and essay in English.

SIREN

In the dead of lockdown,
a siren rips the air
from ambulance to ambulance
from hospital to hospital
like a long gasp for breath.
The sun cannot cut it,
a storm cannot drown it,
the hungry children can't grasp
the death it portends,
and the stray cats and dogs,
like the children, cannot
see the stars up high
for the waters are too murky
to drink, the garbage cans are empty
because restos are closed
and nobody throws anything anymore
for beggars or for homeless animals.

Only the front liners feel and face
the end every minute
trying to save lives.
And prayers grow longer
and longer with the names of those
who succumb to the virus.
In the dead of lockdown,
a siren rips the air
from ambulance to ambulance
from hospital to hospital
like a long, long gasp for breath.

MOFEREFERE LEKOROTSOANA

is a South African poet. His poetry collection, *Shapes Shades and Faces*, was published by African Perspectives Publishers in Johannesburg, South Africa.

CALL OF THE WILD

we ride the midnight in thick fog
with the shortness of breath
and a high fever
the Buffalo at the lead
before time runs out on us.

to die alone
as if you have no one

to be lonely
at the most tender moment
with only the last gasp.

Mercy rides on shoulders of the ocean
floating gently into the City of Angels
to the east she proclaims
blessed are the Queens who mourn
they shall know Comfort
for it is written that
with mercy comes comfort.

the krewes swung through influenza
in the French Quarter
except this time
high fever has ground the Mardi Gras
the old Creole is done making another whistle stop.

we shadow box the unknown
we hold up our guard with elbow greetings
to shield us from the unseen killer punch in the chest
and we wear a mask to conceal our countenance
every step we take
a deadly dance with the invisible.

NIKOLA MADZIROV

is a poet, essayist and translator, born in 1973 in Strumica, Republic of Macedonia, in a family of war refugees from the Balkan Wars. When he was eighteen, the collapse of Yugoslavia prompted a shift in his sense of identity as a writer. He has reinvented himself in a country that felt new but was still nourished by deeply rooted historical traditions. His poems have been translated into more than thirty languages. His book *Relocated Stone* (2007) won the East European Hubert Burda Poetry Award and the Miladinov Brothers Award at the Struga Poetry Evenings festival. Other recognitions include the Xu Zhimo Silver Leaf award for European poetry at King's College, Cambridge. He has received several international fellowships: International Writing Program (IWP) at University of Iowa; DAAD in Berlin; Marguerite Yourcenar in France, IWW in Hong Kong and Civitella Ranieri in Italy.

SEPARATED*

I separated myself from each truth about the beginnings
of rivers, trees, and cities.
I have a name that will be a street of goodbyes
and a heart that appears on X-ray films.
I separated myself even from you, mother of all skies
and carefree houses.
Now my blood is a refugee that belongs
to several souls and open wounds.
My god lives in the phosphorous of a match,
in the ashes holding the shape of the firewood.
I don't need a map of the world when I fall asleep.
Now the shadow of a stalk of wheat covers my hope,
and my word is as valuable
as an old family watch that doesn't keep time.
I separated from myself, to arrive at your skin
smelling of honey and wind, at your name
signifying restlessness that calms me down,
opening the doors to the cities in which I sleep,
but don't live.
I separated myself from the air, the water, the fire.
The earth I was made from
is built into my home.

AFTER US**

One day someone will fold our blankets
and send them to the cleaners

*Translated from the Macedonian by Graham and Peggy Reid.
**Translated from the Macedonian by Graham and Peggy Reid.

to scrub the last grain of salt from them,
will open our letters and sort them out by date
instead of by how often they've been read.

One day someone will rearrange the room's furniture
like chessmen at the start of a new game,
will open the old shoebox
where we hoard pyjama-buttons,
not-quite-dead batteries and hunger.

One day the ache will return to our backs
from the weight of hotel room keys
and the receptionist's suspicion
as he hands over the TV remote control.

Others' pity will set out after us
like the moon after some wandering child.

I SAW DREAMS*

I saw dreams that no one remembers
and people wailing at the wrong graves.
I saw embraces in a falling airplane
and streets with open arteries.
I saw volcanoes asleep longer than
the roots of the family tree
and a child who's not afraid of the rain.
Only it was me no one saw,
only it was me no one saw.

Translated from the Macedonian by Graham and Peggy Reid.

SILENCE*

There is no silence in the world.
Monks have created it
to hear the horses every day
and feathers falling from wings.

**Translated from the Macedonian by Graham and Peggy Reid.*

GOODENOUGH MASHEGO

is an African poet, political activist and artist who has published three volumes of poetry: *Journey With Me, Taste of My Vomit* and *Just Like Space Cookies*. He is a literary adjudicator for the Sol Plaatje EU Poetry Award and the South African Literary Awards. Much of his poetry has appeared in *New Coin, Timbila, Botsotso, Green Dragon, Baobab* and many other anthologies worldwide, as well as on the online platforms *Lit Net* and *Badalisha Poetry Exchange*. He is the winner of the 2016 National Heritage Council Voice of Heritage Award.

LOCKDOWN!

the first letter you read from me be your rude awakening
time you envied no more get on your feet and learn from me
capture every word i write try to fathom the meaning
settle not for 'it was written' see your dreams as precious
pursue with gusto every scheme conceive yours and chase cash

the first five words on the letter 'dear homey on the streets'
take this time to warn ya to increase the peace
let's change the future for posterity growing up was death knell
our dreams shrouded in misfortune failure we dated like girls
i show no love to traitors they're reminders to how i fell

my greetings laced with anecdotes i really miss you from
my heart
the money games we both played though the odds were
against us
our ambitions to clone cash and leave the ghetto behind us
i don't intend to reminisce but your memory's profound
today in self-isolation you're the only hope i got

verse two contains my paranoia, questions to put in the clear
about my girlfriend marilyn and her conduct in my absence
though we met on the battlefield even soldiers taste loneliness
if she stays true to a hustler even when i quarantine alone
last week she called to say 'hi' i sensed betrayal in her voice

in conclusion i wish i had a card or a gift
but now my love is sentimental only this text i give
tried to sneak out buy you flowers got twenty-one more days
for the act
i grew weary of hoping but exercises daily
i peep through my front door catch the mailman daily

eventually I'll jot you letters that's my promise to you
trust in your darkest hour I'll be right there by you
this is the 1st of 100 letters one feeling one verse
one day I'll walk out of here we'll finally twist some trees
sincerely yours; your homeboy in-self isolation.

BISHNU MOHAPATRA

is a well-known Indian poet. He has authored four books of poetry in Odia and has translated two volumes of Pablo Neruda's poetry. A volume of his poetry in English translation, *A Fragile World*, was published in 2005. Bishnu is professor and dean of the School of Interwoven Arts and Sciences of Krea University, Andhra Pradesh, India. He is a political theorist, an educator and a commentator on society, governance, policy and culture.

INTIMACY OF DISTANCE*

These days when my hands meet
they speak in a strange new language.
A foamy, bubbly, bursting,
rising and falling language.
And then, they switch to that
intimate dance
before getting
ready to
separate
again.

At the front door of my apartment
the door knob leaps,
my hand recoils.
I stand in front of a house mirror.
Staring back at me
is that same, old, utterly familiar
distance.

A young worker lies at night,
his face to the sky,
Burning bright like an electric bulb,
Venus hangs, over his head.
So close, he reaches—hand outstretched
and whispers,
'Won't you touch me tonight?'

**Translated from the Odia by the poet with Aparna Uppaluri.*

SONNET MONDAL

is a poet and literary curator based in Kolkata, West Bengal. He is the author of *Karmic Chanting* (Copper Coin Press) and five other books of poetry. Winner of the 2016 Gayatri Gamarsh Memorial Award for literary excellence, he is also a guest editor for *Poetry at Sangam*, and *Words Without Borders*, New York. Sonnet is the founder director of Chair Poetry Evenings International Festival. His poetry has been translated into Hindi, Hungarian, Italian, Slovenian, Spanish, Portuguese, Slovak, Turkish, Macedonian, Bengali and Arabic.

LOCKDOWN

Where roads do not unfurl
the need for limits
breathes through dry tears.

Where solitude takes wing
for the falling sun
amnesia shrouds a generation.

Caged, wingless, a bird waits
for the last dusk

as a forsaken boatman
rows for food in the twilight.

VISHNU NAGAR

is a poet, short-story writer, humourist and journalist. A recipient of several prestigious awards, he has more than fifty books to his credit. His poems have been translated into several Indian as well as foreign languages.

TO THE VILLAGE IN 2020*

Dragged like dust by a storm
They walk
Walk from cities to their village
Like it's 1947 again

People on foot
Hunger on foot
A storm on foot
Bags on foot
Bundles on foot
Bottles full of water on foot

Some barely able to stand
Taking their first steps
Leaving their mother's veil
Now learn of crushing fatigue

Like everyone else
They walk to the village

In the furious sun
They walk
Rains without respite
People without rest
Running from its grip
As hunger stops them

The megacity's bedrock walks away
Its foolish frame laughs

Her daughter walks
My son walks
Bereft of hope

---

* *Translated from the Hindi by Ankur Nagar.*

Keeping in tears
Burning with fever
They walk

Unseen, they walk
For those who look away

It's midnight
They walk
Eyes wish to seek shelter
Feet itch to be tired
Hunger craves a halt
No friendly roof
Not an inch to rest
They walk

The sun will rise
At the village
The sobs will break
At the village
Exhaustion will overwhelm
At the village

Neither beedi in hand
Nor a soothing chai
Still, 800 miles
Will be crossed
The village awaits

A hell left behind
A hell on hand
A sky their own
That was never theirs
The village awaits

The village will be there
For yet another return

The village will be there
For the storm to gather again
And when death arrives
Shrouded by the megacity
The village will disappear

MARC NAIR

is a poet and photographer from Singapore. He has published and edited twelve books of poetry and is the co-founder and principal photographer of *Mackerel*, an online culture magazine. His latest collection is *Sightlines* (2019, Math Paper Press), a collaboration of travel photography and poetry with Tay Tsen-Waye, a film photographer.

COPPER

In those days of unguarded moments,
thieves slipped from shadow to cut holes
in fences, punching through asbestos
and emptied classrooms to pull hallways
of copper wire from false ceilings.

They coiled the copper around
the broken heart of unpaid rent
and the absence of birdsong, rolled
the drums down empty roads towards
a lost port, stopping only for sunrise.

Copper became a dishonest conductor
of greed, its rust-orange lustre
an electric shame, metaphor for what
had been stripped from the world.
We became borders around ourselves,

masking the invisible, only our eyes
said goodbye for missing hours,
for gasping patients and billionaire
islands; in abandon, we had nothing fit
for a eulogy. There are streets

where nobody lives now and we
may no longer love in the same ways.
If we do touch, be fierce; write longing
into each moment, wind around me
like copper, until something sparks again.

MEERA NAIR

is a poet, dancer, actor and writer. Meera's first book of poems, *Grey: Born When Black Invaded White* (Authors Press, 2015), won her the second place at the Muse India Young Writers Award 2015. Meera went on to bring out two more volumes of poetry: *Poetry Vending Machine* (Authors Press, 2016) and *EnBody* (RLFPA Editions, 2019).

INSANITY

It lurked outside the doorstep
Just a call away
It blew flying kisses
And ran away
It beckoned
And then disappeared
You played its game of hide and seek

Through the open window
You could touch the moon
You gathered the moonlight in your arms
And bathed in its ethereal glow

When you woke up to empty mornings
It came visiting
It laid its heavy head on your chest
Trapped, you could hardly breathe

It became stories, poems
Pictures, words
You clutched them to your breast
'Mine, mine,' you said
Till he trampled on them
And called you insane

Locked down
You meet your demon face to face
You embrace it

RAJ NAIR

published his first poem at the age of eleven. He has written poems, short stories and novels in his native language Malayalam and English. He is also a writer-director of feature and documentary films. He was educated at the universities of London, Harvard and Hong Kong. Raj is a professoriate and senior clinician, who lives in Australia.

EASTER*

It is Easter today.

I walked with the silent creatures
who began to chat with me.

Earth makes me listen to the voices
we had forgotten to hear.

Everything should rise from the dead today.

The peacock dances like a rainbow
in the black tar on the road

The peacock commanded me: 'Rise!'

Turtles lay eggs on my salt-laden sand.

The sand commanded me: 'Rise!'

Birds fly down from the sky
to clean my grain-heavy palms

Their wings, now freed from fear,
commanded me: 'Rise!'

The fish in the water
sleep on my toes

The eyes of the sleeping fish
commanded me: 'Rise!'

You and I should not forget
to resurrect today,
said the wayward wind
free from the smell of smoke

Today silent creatures
kept me company during my walk.

** Translated from the Malayalam by K. Satchidanandan.*

TASLIMA NASRIN

is a novelist, poet, essayist, memoirist and human rights activist, originally from Bangladesh. She is known for her writings on women's oppression and her criticism of her religion. She has battled forced exile and multiple fatwas calling for her death. Nasrin's works have been translated into thirty languages. Nasrin has been living in exile since 1994, first in Europe and the United States, and now in India. As a vocal feminist and human rights activist, she has won numerous awards and fellowships. These include the Sakharov Prize from the European Parliament; the Academy Award from the Royal Academy of Arts, Science and Literature of Belgium; Edict of Nantes Prize from the city of Nantes, France; Kurt Tucholsky Prize by Swedish PEN; honorary doctorate from Paris Diderot University, France; and the Simone de Beauvoir Prize and the Human Rights Award from the Government of France.

WE*

Last night a lizard sprang from nowhere and landed along my arm, then climbed upon my shoulder before inching towards my head and hiding itself in the dishevelled bush of my hair. Resting under that nest, it gawks at a second lizard for what must be hours. At dawn, it slides next to my ear before deciding to squat upon my spine. The second lizard, frozen upon my right leg around two inches below my knee, feels my pulse there. Neither moves from their positions the entire day, the entire evening. Me? I did what I normally do. I kept lying with my eyes firmly closed. Silently—and even if there's really no rationale whatsoever for counting in reverse—I counted from one hundred to one, one hundred to one, one hundred to one, one hundred to one...

My bed is a confused mess of dirty clothes, cracked bowls with leftover meals on used trays; notebooks for scribbling, old newspapers turned brown because of tea; a comb with stray, grey hairs sticking to them; one or two sad puffed rice crackers; scattered strips of pills and potion phials; inkless pens.

For a number of days, more than two hundred black ants have occupied my bed. Millimetre by millimetre, they have girded up their loins to construct a new colony inside me, digging tunnels for days on end. I myself have become as tiny as these ants. I'm utterly stunned, watching their performance of *Giselle* upon the surface of my body—but not once have I been bitten or summoned, even by mistake.

I wonder which of us belongs to the other. Perhaps I'm safer with them, without us.

**Translated from the Bengali by Samik Bandyopadhyay and Jesse Waters.*

BAN'YA NATSUISHI

is a Japanese poet and director of the Modern Haiku Association in Japan. He has also co-founded the international haiku magazine *Ginyu* (Troubadour). He has published eight haiku collections, including *The Diary of Everyday Hunting* (1983), *Rhythm in the Vacuum* (1986), *The Fugue of Gods* (1990), *Opera in the Human Body* (1990), *Earth Pilgrimage* (1998) and the English-language edition of *A Future Waterfall* (1999). He has also edited *Guide to 21st Century Haiku* (1997).

HAIKU

The invisible crown
makes everything
vacant

SOPHIA NAZ

is a bilingual poet, essayist, author, editor and translator. She has been nominated twice for the Pushcart Prize. Her work appears in numerous literary journals, including *Poetry International Rotterdam*, *The Adirondack Review*, *The Wire*, *Chicago Quarterly Review*, *Blaze Vox*, *Scroll*, *The Daily O*, *Cafe Dissensus*, *Guftugu*, *Pratik*, *Gallerie International*, *Coldnoon*, *VAYAVYA*, *The Bangalore Review* and *Madras Courier*. She is author of the poetry collections *Peripheries* (2015), *Pointillism* (2017) and *Date Palms* (2017). *Shehnaz*, a biography of her mother, was published by Penguin Random House in November 2019.

(G)HOST

Just a moment, the old gods say
We are coming to lateness, silence
shadow-shawled, do you not see

Our symmetry scrawled in your mirror? Grave
length two handspans wide, while you pace
let us place our diadems, so . . .

Lost in your address, gods!
there's no end to its numinous mucus
scolding star scaffolding

Dancing cheek to cheek with a night
of numberless hours; clock face, no hands
holding long knives of dream

Reins making reliquary clot while you talk
oceans, mouth-froth, thick spackle on
mortuary walls, corridors of wasted youth

Tell me again how paradise was lost
in a poisonous smile
infected blanket

I'm lying here, pinned to your story
gullible Gulliver
while Lilliput takes over

Is not sleep next of kin
to death? Sing me
a lullaby, gods

Again from your mouths of stone

KAI MICHAEL NEUMANN

is a German poet. He has lived in several countries, including the US, the UK, South Africa, and now in Spain. He is a general medical practitioner and also holds a PhD in Medicine.

A LAST AND LASTING ACORN

Deep within impermanence and continuity of change
Seeds lie shielded waiting and protected for the moment
They trust that the cupid cupule holds the bow and arrows
Firmly based in the grasp of nature and uncharted destiny

Sheltered for the generation of life's resilient circulation
Encased in a rough nutshell of inevitable wheels of life
Resides with un-shattered purpose a simple magic miracle
A gem more powerful than the chronicle of human nature

One day she says I'll be a forest in the sprouting aspiration
Of hope and kindness that spread with wind and fortune
The elements will nurture me until I'm ready to stand tall
For now I must be grateful for my budding tender youth

I don't grow fast but when my roots grip potent undergrowth
My canopy gives wings to dreams and certitude of aspirations
Love is the meaning of the fertile soil gracing my surroundings
Founded in heaven I grant my strength to future generations

Equipped with a kernel of truth and change along the lineage
Core and essence transform vile lies from the sediment of time
Sometimes you close your eyes and trample on my saplings
But I'm a survivor and take care knowing that I'm truly loved

Surely you can cut the branches and try to break my promise
Craft treasure chests or dressers from my hardened resolve
Put another log on the fire and watch me rising from hot ashes
Build turrets for your fortresses of power and castles onto sand

Sometimes I drift in raging waters unable to steer my voyage
Float in the ocean and yet when spring resumes I'm here again
Smoothed and ground in the knowledge that my acorns live
Whatever weather may embrace my nascent children's fate

I can't complain for when I hand over the torch and novelty
When I'm old and felled down to size by turbulence and storms
I can rest assured that fires and drought did not snuff my passion
And that my final passage opens opportunities from start to end

BARBARA OPPENHEIMER

is an American poet and a retired social worker whose poetry reflects her interest in contemporary social problems, including the unequal distribution of justice and income and healthcare. Her empathy for the underprivileged is evident in her poetry which often involves the downtrodden and the mentally ill. She has won three local awards and has published through Amazon.

PARADISE LANE

smells of mulch, new mown grass
two Mercedes parked in a row

lacrosse sticks lean on shiny bikes
plastic shovels strewn on walk

gardeners sit on curb
lunch on laps

masked passing joggers smile
nod, sometimes wave

noting miles on watchbands they
give a wide berth to port-a-potties

garbage trucks roll by, man swings
off fast, grabs trashcans, heaves,

runs to the next house, grabs
heaves, stops, breathes hard

red Mercedes backs up
honks loud at workers,

turns right, drives off
radio blares

DEFENCE

Fifty years ago they said
the bullet might have his name on it
they said
it might be his time to die
the man understands
that war is history

this war cruel, invasive,
helpless victims multiply
cease to breathe
hospital beds emptied,
refrigerated trucks lined up
ready for their cargo

in mud between buildings
the man crouches
moulds wet dirt
into ridges
forms a tiny staircase
each step
perfectly level

AMIR OR

is an Israeli poet, novelist and essayist, and the 2020 Golden Wreath laureate. His works have been published in fifty languages.

CAMERA OBSCURA*

Darkness doesn't distinguish between things,
doesn't recognize you
except by your voice wandering among the echoes;
by the sour smell of your fear, by your desire
to rip your image out of the darkness
to rip a shadow for yourself out of the shadows.

Darkness is a womb without walls—
there's only myself inside myself.
In the dark locked room a child learns
to listen, touch, be
pulse and skin.

REFLECTION**

These are reflections that became frozen forever.
This is the mirror room of memory:
A child in the darkness
plays hide and seek with shadows
sinks into the secret places of the stairs
turns into shadow.
A child in the darkness
separates from his image
dreams his face inwards.
In a mirror of darkness
he reveals light—
and sees.

---

*Written bilingually in Hebrew and English.
**Written bilingually in Hebrew and English.

SEVEN LINES TO SUNRISE*

And despite it all—life; despite it all—love.
We'll indeed see the heart's gate
open to a world of hope.
In its paths we'll stride again, wondering at its beauty,
our spirits clear and peaceful:
we'll indeed see the rising morning,
the coming sunrise of Man.

Translated from the Hebrew by Seth Michelson.

* Translated from the Hebrew by Seth Michelson.

HARRY OWEN

is an English-born poet. In 2008, he moved to South Africa from the UK where he had been appointed the inaugural Poet Laureate for Cheshire in 2003. Outspoken in his commitment to the natural world and a passionate advocate of poetry, he is the author of eight collections, the three most recent being *Small Stones for Bromley* (Lapwing Publications, Belfast, 2014); *The Cull: New and Resurrected Poems* (The Poets Printery, East London, 2017); and *All Weathers* (The Ink Sword, Grahamstown, 2019).

GESTATION

Sure as babies,
nine months down the line
there'll be a boom
of virus poems.

No one will ask
Do you remember
what you were doing when . . .?
because we'll all know:

the wailing and teething,
the semantic nappy-changing
will be quite
unmistakable

UNHINGED AT CHINTSA

After the great windstorm that blew in from the West—
sunshine and luminous skies disowning the gale's treachery
of amputated branches, dust and dune-menacing surf—

he dreams in the calm of another day, glances out
from his book through ageing French windows
across the sundeck to a newly crisp ocean, rich

as the skirling of pipes beyond silverleaf, milkwood,
strelitzia and palm: he knows this pulsing
creature, this loved world, as he knows his own breath.

As he stares, the open door groans, creaks back on itself,
subsides in a heap—a stricken glass geriatric
crutched and straining for support. Years of salt air

have rotted the old screws, and he hadn't noticed.
Quick to grab the frame and hold it up,
they wedge it clumsily back into place,

locking it in. It will hold for a few more days, they hope.
But who will restore this fragile thing now
in such a time of keening collapse?

Suddenly the whole bright world is unhinged.
It needs fixing.

SAY SOMETHING

about us

about scarcity, squalor, disease
about avarice, lust and massacre
about bloodshed, torture, crime
about celebrity, ignorance and bling
about politics

say something

about Syria
Libya, Afghanistan
say something about Nairobi
and a thousand other wretched places

say something

about war

say something

about sweat shops, jobs and slavery
about poisoning, pollution and pimps
about fracking the Karoo

the obscene nonsense of sustainable growth
about things that waste and die
that we're killing along with ourselves
about China

say something

about elephant, rhino and lion
about tiger, orang-utan, pangolin
condor, dolphin and whale
say something about the planet
our lovely threatened globe
about me, about me, about ours
about us

say something

about sickness of the body
of the TV mind
of the right to speak out
of the heart, of the soul
about death
about death
about death

say something

about husbands
wives and daughters
about sisters, brothers, sons
say something about corruption
about murder and rape
about loneliness, sorrow
wickedness, despair

say something about gods and gullibility
about faith, about bigotry

and sin
about daydreams and night terrors
the childish compulsion to believe . . .

. . . then pause
and say something

if you can (whisper it)
about peace, about hope, about life
say something, something
about them, about us
the same, we're the same
some honour, some decency
some light, some love

not gods, not spirits
not heavens, not hells

but us

us alone

something, Some Thing

that we are

speak it and speak it and speak it:
speak us

JOSE PADUA

is the author of *A Short History of Monsters*, which was chosen by former Poet Laureate Billy Collins as the winner of the 2019 Miller Williams Poetry Prize and is now out from the University of Arkansas Press. His poetry, fiction and non-fiction have appeared in publications such as *Bomb*, *Salon.com*, *Beloit Poetry Journal*, *Exquisite Corpse*, *Another Chicago Magazine*, *Unbearables*, *Crimes of the Beats*, *Up is Up, but So Is Down: New York's Downtown Literary Scene, 1974-1992*, and others. He has written features and reviews for *Salon*, *The Weeklings*, *NY Press*, *Washington City Paper*, the *Brooklyn Rail* and *The New York Times*, and has read his work at Lollapalooza, CBGBs, the Knitting Factory, the Public Theater, the Living Theater, the Nuyorican Poets' Café, the St Mark's Poetry Project, and many other venues. He was a featured reader at the 2012 Split This Rock poetry festival and won the New Guard Review's 2014 Knightville Poetry Prize.

HIGH

My response to the current plague is to wake up
a little later each morning. The kids are home
from school and don't need to go anywhere, don't
need to learn anything, at least not right now.
Because what is there to learn during a crisis
except how to stay alive, keep your heart beating
like a disco song? I remember the '70s, remember
being so impressed by the beautiful colour speed
came in. Those beautiful old days when my legs
could still take me to far places. I go to sleep
early now, lie down when I'm tired, don't stay up late
writing poems and stories listening to Pharoah Sanders,
the New York Dolls, or Disco Tex and the Sexolettes.
Holy Christ was that a song, or was that a sign
that someone was glad to see me since the last manifestation
of apocalyptic ennui? I walk slowly down the stairs now
in deference to my arthritic knees, aware that my sense
of balance is something like a hit of acid, those long-ago
nights when I'd look at people without nodding
even more than when I wasn't on acid, or mushrooms.
Oh what a feeling that was, oh what a way to feel
the non-ache and flexing muscle around my
Filipino-American or sometimes just American
young bones, and bones seem more important now,
like the bone-in pork at the grocery store, which I go to
wearing a mask, mittens, goggles and galoshes
because I like that alliterative ambiance. I like the way
a man is a man and a woman is a woman and a they
is a they doing it so gloriously for theyselves
or I mean themselves, or whatever safe space selves.
I eat quickly now like a meal is a moment so easily
stolen from you, watching the evening news

while taking slow gulps from my glass of cold water,
so far from those days when we drank Schlitz
or Michelob and thought Coors was the ultimate beer
when nowadays we say, oh seriously, fuck Coors
and fuck beer. I want craft brew with a hint
of cardamom and orange peel, served in a mug
that bears the logo of my favourite non-profit organization.
Treat me like my name is Bill Murray and my middle name
is Fucking. Believe in me like my name is Don Corleone
and it's the first half of *The Godfather*, before he got old. But
my name is Jose Padua and my pronouns are motherfucker,
motherfucker and motherfucker's. How did it end up like this
in these horse's rear-end times? Why do I have to translate
for you my existential bewilderments? Why am I on the
bullet train back from New York when my friends are
riding coach, I guess I'm lucky that way. And I'm amazed
at how my son from such a young age made sure to describe
the precise thing he wanted like ice-cold water or a cream
cheese sandwich, make sure not to cut it in half 'cause that
sucks; how my daughter paints pictures of things the way
she sees them, stripped of the spectacle of corporate costume,
entrance music and colour scheme; how my wife stands so long
like a walk through a garden when it's a house we live in and
not the open earth under a starry distant sky between river
and mountain. Right before the plague we packed up that
old house out in small-town America. Half our neighbours
were crazed, the other half wholesome as the virgin breath
of infants; they made shelter from an atmosphere of rolling
coal and diesel fuel. I think it was Guy Debord who said
it's so much easier for mainstream media to cover a brand
than a genuine human being. Either that or me in a dream
where I'm smart and lucid and have read every paragraph
Guy Debord ever wrote in the original French. My name
is Jose Padua, it's just a name I'm saying again because

this is a time of modern plague and shit. It's a time of
plague and they're asking us to choose between
the lesser piece of shit and the worst piece of shit. Then
telling us that if we hold out for something better,
we're a piece of shit, too. I remember humanity before
it became nothing more than an empty shell; then I remember
that humanity was always an empty shell. Every moment
the memory's different. So we take the kids out back,
bounce the ball around or throw it in the alley away from
everyone else. Look up at the wires on telephone poles,
the loose strands that keep us connected to other faces
and ways of life. I hear a voice in the distance saying
something I can't understand. And footsteps which
means to leave them some space, let them go on their
way like disarmed enemies. This is America 2020 and
I feel like I'm back on acid again. Staring at people,
my head still as a traffic signal. Blinking, flashing,
shining colour as if to say, yeah, move on, and call me
motherfucker. And up above us it's a cloudy sky. And
the birds are flying, they're keeping their distance from
one another, making dark wide circles in the scraping air
as they fly so beautifully high, so beautifully high.

DIANE WILBON PARKS

is a poet, visual artist and author. Diane has published two poetry collections, including *The Wisdom of Blue Apples*. She is an honoree of Prince George's County Poets of Excellence. She celebrated the permanent installation of one of her poems and artwork at the Patuxent Research Refuge, North Tract, near Fort Meade, Maryland. She has been featured on Grace Cavalieri's 'The Poet and The Poem' at the Library of Congress, as well as Prince George's CTV's award-winning programme, *Sojourn with Words*. Diane is the founder of The Write Blend, a poetry ensemble of six culturally diverse poets. She holds a degree in Information Systems Management and is a senior IT program manager and an US Air Force Veteran. She resides in Maryland with her husband, son, daughter and dog, Cooper.

ISOLATED WINGS

We are snowed in, in spring,
listening to indulgence from the chirps of birds,
fluttering feet and faces of sun-drenched homes rising,
opening the gold of blue skies.
The world props against windows and doors,
wishing for wings and the songs of birds.

For more than forty days,
we've been flying into windows,
with untrained wings,
caged—inside walls,
inside oily fingerprints left on glass.
I keep wiping the edges of you off
cleaning the traces of your
wild baby's breath,
now marred with Lysol.

April cringes inside its bloom,
afraid to lurk beyond
its curled-tongue, leaflet buds.
Windows listen for
wind-rushed, poetic mewlings,
the colour of dance
is a strong song,
wept in a brush of uncut grass
and the husk of sycamore trees;
sleeves of rice bleed grain by grain,
we eat sparingly.

We see a man dancing
in the centre of the earth
with meat skins, whistling sound like flutes,
these isolated, iridescent wings can't fly

even fish feathers into water—life is still a flutter,
paddled fins wade in waters that still flow
and, the mist of white clouds, return blue.

The world props
against cheeks and chests,
windows lick the oily salt of our skin,
while fingers flap in and out of dreams
unmasked words wish to be free again.

With outstretched wings,
we lift our opens,
point our perched bodies to the wind;
we twist our cages and bend them back
while the cageless man still dances in the feathers of his skin.

SABINE PASCARELLI

is an Italian poet from Tuscany, near Florence. She grew up in Germany where she earned a degree in German language and literature at Dortmund University. She is a published poet, an author of children's literature and a translator of English, German and Italian. Her recent books of translated poems include *The Alchemy of Grief* by Emily Ferrara, winner of the Bordighera Poetry Award 2007, *Repubblica* by Dr J.H. Beall and *Cosa farei per amore* by Grace Cavalieri.

20 MAY 2020

I watch the behaviour of the people on the street.
A variety of stories lie hidden behind the protecting
masks. Is this the end of trust? Eyes don't meet
eyes. Hands pointing to the ground, empty of gestures.
Feet moving in silence.

The young woman working in the studio of an architect
takes off her mask to greet me. *How are you?* Without
waiting for my answer, she assures me of how well she is,
eyes contradicting lips. *Times are tough for so many,*
she adds, her voice is a balance of fear and control.

I wish I could say something of comfort, as she walks away.
Half down the street I see her speak to someone else.
Aimless love keeps us in its claws, I think.
I don't know how this sentence comes to me.

LET US

break the rules   quarantine out the heartless and the
    mean   care for them until they recover

they don't know how contagious they are   how loved   they
    may cough at us

not intelligent   as a virus   acting without good or
    bad   to find fertile soil the only intention

let us   break the rules   in the laboratories   of our
    hearts secretly

create a virus   set it free   we are many   undercover
    potent voice

softly speaking

ANURADHA PATIL

is a well-known Marathi poet from Aurangabad, Maharashtra. She has five collections of poems to her credit: *Digant* (1981), *Tarieehee* (1985), *Divasendivas* (1992), *Waluchya Patrat Mandlela Khel* (2005) and *Kadaachit Ajunahi* (2017). Her poems have been translated into many Indian languages and have won a number of awards. In 2019, she received the Sahitya Akademi Award (for *Kadaachit Ajunahi*) and the Vinda Karandikar Lifetime Achievement honour from the Government of Maharashtra.

MIGRATION DURING LOCKDOWN*

In this world of jugglers
Once again
Their cracked feet are treading the path
For miles and miles
Of a new partition
With the extinguished eyes,
Turning into a living legend.

Neither the humans nor the trees
Grow overnight
Out of the dust
They have neither a past nor a future
Only the present accompanies them
Wherever they go
To crush their dreams

Saying that these days will also pass
They fold their legs to the stomach
And sleep at the roadside
While telling the story
Of a roti for tomorrow
To the constantly crying children

They are unaware of
The green branch taking roots
And the roots sprouting from the roots
Growing overwhelmingly
In the direction of life
But they know it intuitively
That all cannot drink the dazzling moonlight

---

* *Translated from the Marathi by Dileep V. Chavan.*

By mixing it in the water
And all cannot see the dawn
After the deluge
Blooming on our horizon
Where even a mute piece of a roti
Slips from the hand suddenly
Then a dense black forest
Grows within them

K.G. SANKARA PILLAI

retired as principal, Maharaja's College, Kochi. He has eleven collections of poems in Malayalam and has been translated into various Indian and foreign languages. He is the author of two books of essays, two books of interviews and one travelogue. His many awards include the Sahitya Akademi Award.

WHERE IS THE END OF IT?*

Dear Old Shark,
is there a hook hanging above my head?
It pricks while moving.
The wave caresses, as if to kiss.

My serene morning strolls,
blocked by cyclones and threats.
In the open and closed narratives of water,
I meet fear, war, hunger and death.
Peace was my choice of safe distance
from the extremes.

Unable to fly high or dive deep,
our folk sails in the chaos:
having no destination,
having no addition to our credits.
I face the dim surface of being.
I fail to be a fish in the water.

Tell me dear friend,
is there a hook
hanging above my head?

Yes, beloved Lady Shark.
There is a hook hanging above
your head, my head, every head—
the greedy beak of
the invisible vulture in the gallows.

I hear fear as a silent roar,
far and wide.
Where is the end of it?

---

* *Translated from the Malayalam by Aditya Shankar and the poet.*

MASK*

Procured bread, egg, mask and coconuts.
Maintained balance clarity in my phone.

Locked the world away upon reaching home.

Alongside the shopping bag,
secured the unruptured, unscathed hope
that I need even tomorrow.

Washed hands off injustice,
even one delivered by a microbe.
Changed. Put my feet up.

The 'I' who reclines is
the remnant of what Bangalore pickpocketed,
the remnant of what Bangalore rescued,
the remnant of stolen consciousness,
the remnant of a masked mouth and nose.
An online creature, distance-vowed.

For me,
the inside is inside,
the outside is outside
from now on.

Won't come again, again
(Oh, won't it, won't it?)
that bygone time when we were one
and relished travelling together.
Won't come again,
our tale of unity that yielded several gains.

---

* *Translated from the Malayalam by Aditya Shankar and the poet.*

A wave of stench in the air.
Was I sold a rotten egg, a stale bread,
a rancid oil, a foul hope?

What stinks?
Is it the mind that craves for everything?
Or a house that turns everything old?
Or a dungeon that hides in a home?
Is it the ailing world?

Does the stink of fear spread outside
from the decaying inside?
Or does it spread within from the decaying outer?

Knock. Knock. Impatient
many hands knock on the door,
many legs kick on the chest.
Is it the desperate return of the enslaved workforce
from their failed exodus to an imagined swaraj?
Without a Moses or a Marx or a Gandhi
to wield a magic wand and lead,
Is it the furious whirlwind of the wretched of the Earth?

An enraged query at the door:

'Who is inside?'
'The house owner, the card holder.
The authorized citizen.
A language, a poet, a ration-eater,
fretting about an uncertain future.'

'Who is outside?'
'Corona.'

JERRY PINTO

is a Mumbai-based Indian writer and journalist. His works include *Helen: The Life and Times of an H-Bomb* (2006), which won the Best Book on Cinema Award at the 54th National Film Awards, *Surviving Women* (2000) and *Asylum and Other Poems* (2003). He won the Sahitya Akademi Award for his first novel, *Em and the Big Hoom* (2012).

LEARNING

From Dust

The fan needs cleaning.
On top of each blade, a thick layer of dirt.
I think of the first particle of dust that settled there.
When the fan started it must have been whirled off.
Nevertheless it persists.
Dust gathers.
It sticks together.
Dust hangs on.
Can I learn from dust?

From Ants

I set a plate down: cheese, tomato, boiled egg.
A black ant comes along, another, another.
Good times, good times, food, they say to each other.
Mountains of food.
All along the chain the message passes:
Mountains of protein, mountains of food.
I take my plate away.
The ants are perplexed.
Food? Mountain of food?
Where did it go?
Didn't you say . . .? Didn't we hear . . .?
A second later they're all searching again.
For other food. Other mountains.
Can I learn from ants?

From Swabbing

The first day I crouched to swab;
Because that's the best way, everyone says;
Because the best maids squat to swab, everyone knows.
My knees groaned all night.
The second day, I swabbed standing.
The third day, I decided swabbing
Every day was not really necessary.
Every alternate day will do it.
Can I be master to the maid
That I am to myself?

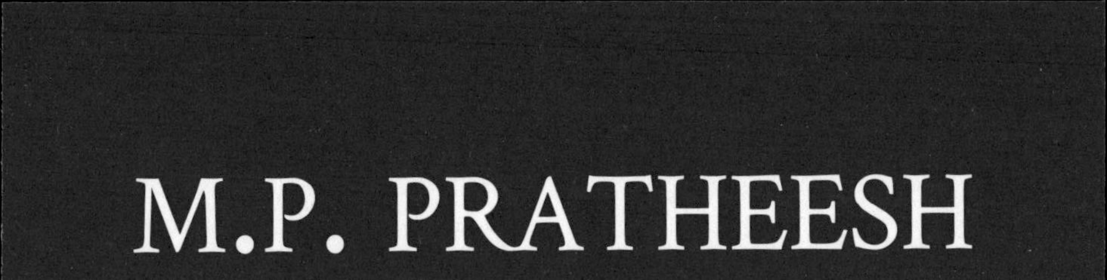
M.P. PRATHEESH

GRIEF*

A tree stands alone
on the courtyard behind the house.
The grief of being alone
hangs heavy on its leaves.

A blue butterfly flutters around,
chats and plays with the tree,
pulls its hair, laughs

The grief of the lonely tree
flies off, dissolves and disappears
somewhere inside the breeze.

THE MISSING MAN**

A man used to live
in a narrow room on the street
like sweat spread over a tissue,
his words stuck to the
curves of pots and pans:
a man so small that
you could see him if you
just scratched them with your nails
or rubbed them with force.

I thought I heard someone say
at his funeral that he used to write poetry;
I couldn't get it clear in the noise
of the red earth falling on him.

---

* *Translated from the Malayalam by K. Satchidanandan.*
** *Translated from the Malayalam by K. Satchidanandan.*

SAVITHRI RAJEEVAN

is a noted Malayalam poet and short-fiction writer, based in Thiruvananthapuram, Kerala. She won the Kerala Sahitya Akademi Award for Poetry in 2018 for her widely read collection of poetry in Malayalam, *Ammaye Kulippikumbol*. Her poetry is celebrated for its sophisticated imagery devoid of ornamentation. The themes of her poems stretch wide and borrow from experience, observation, art and political history. Her works have been anthologized in many Indian and foreign publications across many languages.

GRAVITY*

O tell me, what pulls you to earth?
I am sure, you will not say
It's the greenery, the breeze, the river,
Or this night of the enchanting blue moon

I hear you say, there was something
That exists no more
I hear you say, you lost it
In the depths of the past
Diving deep in its abyss
Swimming in its vast expanse,
You say you are not able to retrieve
What you once lost.

Yet,
Why do you remain bound to this earth?
Is it the howls from the hell that you hear?
In your prayers, in the dark
Did you suddenly see the Hell
In Heironymus Bosch's painting
Look back at you?
Their macabre laments
Emanating from parched lands
Scorched skies
And dried-up throats?

Your eyes that lost their sparkle,
Lips that forgot to blossom into a smile
and weary sighs

They whisper to me,
That your present does not hold you close to this earth

**Translated from the Malayalam by Pooja Sagar.*

Yet, you pretend that someone needs you
That he is calling you
To search, give or take something.

You linger
In this present
Listening to the murmur of the seismic waves
Trapped in the earth's gravity.

LIGHT THE LAMP, LIGHT THE LAMP*

Holding on to fever's thin thread
Walking slowly, softly, it came
With no shawl, no umbrella cover
No anklet's tinkle.
In early dawn
The moon still up,
And, on the branch
The lone hooting owl
Had seen this coming.

The moon stretched its arm radiant
Through the window and touched
The sleepless mother.
Mother opened her palm to me:
Is it not full moon tonight?
The moonshine is strangely cool!

Clutching fever's yellow thread
It stood at the door

** Translated from the Malayalam by Dr P. Udaya Kumar.*

With no unfurled mane of golden red
No form or smell or colour.

Before the temple's morning hymns
And the mosque's prayer-call
To wake up my mother
As on every day, came
Night birds to the windowsill.
'Light the lamp, light the lamp,'
Said they in hasty sing-song.
Gods, in their chamber,
Stood in the dark.

At that moment,
Shadowless as a breeze
It entered the room
Alongside the fever.
It was then it cut
In an instant, noiselessly
As if of a new-born babe
My mother's umbilical cord
Tethered to the gods
Waiting for her to light the lamp
To earth, water and wind
To trees birds, humans
To the date, the seasons and the year

That was too the instant
When mother said to me
Like the little bird which
Came and went from the window:
'Light the lamp, light the lamp.'

E.V.
RAMAKRISHNAN

is a bilingual Indian writer and translator. He has published four volumes of poetry in English: *Being Elsewhere in Myself* (1980), *A Python in a Snake Park* (1994), *Terms of Seeing: New and Selected Poems* (2006) and *Tips for Living in an Expanding Universe* (2017). Among his recent critical works in English are *Indigenous Imaginaries: Literature, Region, Modernity* (2017) and *Locating Indian Literature: Texts, Traditions, Translation* (2011). He has received the Kerala Sahitya Akademi Award and Odakkuzhal Award for literary criticism in Malayalam.

BLANK PAGE

I keep vigil at the riverbank.
The night says: I am here.
The river says nothing.

The moon dredges the riverbed.
A giant tusker's shadow
emerges from the wreckage of the river.

Silence and water.

UNTITLED

Erase yourself. You are one too many.
Keep the essential you
on a single parchment. Unwritten.

Be the thread in the needle.
Stitch yourself into something strange.

Like a thatched house,
you should last only for one monsoon.

OTTERS

Otters taught me how to be:
there is no need to be seen to see oneself.

Man was a rumour they did not
believe in. They were sea-conscious
of larger things that stretched beyond
the clock and the calendar.

As I turned away from them,
the crowded seashore became desolate
like a vandalized mausoleum.

YASHODHARA RAY CHAUDHURI

is a poet from Kolkata, India. She has published seventeen collections of poetry and seven collections of prose. She received the Krittibas Puroskar in 1998 and the Pashchim Banga Bangla Akademy's Anita Sunilkumar Basu Award in 2006. She is a member of the prestigious Indian Audit and Accounts Service. Yashodhara is also a translator from French.

I'LL GO HOME*

Swarms of waves come, to tell her—let's go home, let's go home
Slivers of the sun, that peep through the mellow blue sky
Tell her: Let's go home, please, let's go home

Her lover's warm hands in a tender moment
They tempted her with the dream of a home
Let's go home, let's go home, let's go home

The banks, keeled over, sink in her sleep
Hold on to the fragile ropes, cross the bamboo pool
an edged river, jagged rocks, washed away
But cross it, and you are home

In her sleep, flames surround her
The sky splits with lightning
An old homelessness fans and awakens a new one
It parts a way, and leaves
I am a refugee again, on the streets
I return, in tears, to beg
I'll go home, I'll go home, I'll go home.

**Translated from the Bengali by Chirayata Chakrabarty.*

KUTTI REVATHI

is an Indian poet, recognized as possessing a vital new idiom both within the poetics and politics of the Tamil literary tradition and in that borderless space we now think of as 'world poetry'. She is well-known for bringing out the passionate poetical effervescence of a woman's psycho-physic pursuits. She is the author of thirteen poetry collections, including the controversial *Mulaigal*, and three collections of short fiction. She is now composing lyrics for Oscar-winning music composer A.R. Rahman and has directed her debut Tamil feature film, *Siragu* (2019).

A MIRROR, AS AN ENTRANCE*

1. *The Rotation of a Clock*

Where has gone the bloodstream of that fury?
Where have they gone,
those screams of hatred, that scorch the ears?
Left to themselves,
why do these clock-hands of the present
rotate staying so wide apart from one another?
The Earth had many a reason
for its long-needed rest.
Amidst the forest fires,
And the tsunamis and the drowning mountains,
A moment's freedom from the groans of suffering.
But, the face I had enjoyed looking in the mirror,
On it was stuck my time like a blotch.

2. *Isolation*

I left you at a distance,
beneath the sunlight, looking like a fluorescent pond.
Your eyes' anxieties snowballed
And ran after me on the road.
What my eyes had looked at with dread,
on my way back, I had not shared with you.
Though all roads connect us, I know,
all the kisses become dry
at their elongating distances.
While it was possible to fold every other thing
into words and spread them over
to dry in the summer's open space,

**Translated from the Tamil by Ethiraj Akilan.*

the heavy kisses alone remain swooned
in the sacks of loneliness.
As I submit everything to the hands of time,
this day turns to be a sweet one.

3. *Desire*

Desire feels hungry.
Hunger and pain unite.
Grief turns blue.
The oceanic ebbs of loneliness
double up and rise, double up and rise
and touch the peak of mountains.
The focused face glows
like sunshine.
After strains and struggles inside the nostrils
the first breath opens eyes.
The hunger of desire shakes
and pleasure turns blue
akin to grief.

WILLEM M. ROGGEMAN

is a well-known Flemish poet who lives in Brussels. He has been called, by an important critic, 'a painter with words'. It is indeed painting which has had the most influence on his poetry. A professional journalist and art critic, and a former director of the Flemish Cultural Centre De Brakke Grond in Amsterdam, Roggeman also writes novels, plays and essays about Dutch literature and Flemish painters.

THE LONELINESS OF AN OBJECT*

Now that the party's over
it's conspicuous how silence falls
on every object left behind
heavier than ever before.
Now that everyone's left for home
it sits there, alone and useless.
No one still around to look at it,
to touch it or to use it,
find it beautiful or gaudy.

Each object has its unique place
to which it grows attached in time.
But when it's left alone, its meaning
disappears, it's robbed of potency,
impassive and incapable of motion

Left behind in time,
alone and abandoned in the space
of this room, without significance
until someone lifts it up again,
gives it renewed purpose,
calls it by its name
and thus restores it, makes it pristine.

There's nothing quite as lonely
as an object left behind.
All things depend on us for their existence.
When we look at them, they're there.
When we close our eyes, they're not.

Only what we see exists.
And everything we touch or hold

---

* *Translated from the Dutch by Brian Doyle.*

prepares itself, gets ready
for the loneliness awaiting it.

POEM FOR ULRIKE MEINHOF*

Some can't take it anymore.
Some paint a mirror on the wall
with the face of a woman in it.
Some listen to a tape
with the voice of a woman
whose whispering can hardly be heard.
Some feed their imagination
with recollections of adventures
they never experienced.
Some see in the creases
of the blanket on the bed
the shape of a sleeping woman.
Some fall asleep
with one hand in the hand of the night.
Some whisper I love you
and listen to the stove's answer.
Some can't agree with themselves.
Some know the precise personal description
of a woman they never knew.
Some point to the place
where alcohol gave birth to beauty.
Some sit motionless in a room
and travel with dizzying speed
through the country that begins behind the mirror.

---

* *Translated from the Dutch by Brian Doyle.*

Some are afraid of the sunrise.
Some answer the questions
that no one ever asked them
due to lack of interest.
Some see in the wallpaper
how life passes by.
Some can't even talk to themselves.
Some don't realize that yesterday has never begun.
Some sink like stones into time.
Some feel their blood stop running.
No one is alone in his loneliness.

GABRIEL ROSENSTOCK

is an Irish poet, playwright, haikuist, tankaist, essayist and author/translator of over 180 books, mostly in Irish. He has edited and contributed to books of haiku in Irish, English, Scots and Japanese. He is a prolific translator into Irish of international poetry, plays and songs. He is the author of twenty poetry collections in Irish and eleven in English, besides books of essays. He was former chairman of Poetry Ireland, and member, Aosdána, the Irish academy of arts and literature.

COVID-19: THE GENERAL SPEAKS OF HIS SORROW

Self-isolation . . .
These bitter days
When can I send battalions
Of raw young men
To war
To crush their bones
And the bones of others
When will I see them again
Marching proudly
Shoulder to shoulder
Self-isolation . . .
These bitter days
The flash of bayonets
Is no more

HAIKU

smothered
by a protective mask . . .
the laughter of children

SABITHA SATCHI

has been publishing her poems in English and Malayalam from the age of fifteen. She received the Vyloppilli Memorial Sreerekha Award for Poetry in 1991. She has been the recipient of awards and fellowships, including the Paul Mellon Fellowship at Yale University, USA (2014), the Commonwealth Scholarship, UK (2011-17) for research in art history at University College London, the Graduate School Award, University College London (2014), the Sarai-CSDS Independent Fellowship (2003) and the Charles Wallace Fellowship, British Council (2002). Sabitha has been a member of the ongoing Afro-Asia project of poetry and music, Insurrections Ensemble, based in Cape Town, South Africa, since 2011. Her poems have appeared in several reputed journals and anthologies. Sabitha's book of poems, *Hereafter*, is forthcoming from Poetrywala, Mumbai. She lives in Delhi.

EXODUS–IV

(From the series, 'Exodus')

Leftover

A snake slithers, water rises in the boat
Silver fins flicker and flash, raised oars
slash borders with swift cuts, he sets afloat
on the river the choking dread as more
lines are cut, oars take another river's
name in notes of komalgaandhaar, a wail

rises, where is home, where my dancing village
green, where the seemul tree's mottled refuge
on my front yard? He carries walls on his head—
left over in his bundle are just lines of a boat.

EXODUS–V

(From the series, 'Exodus')

Redemption Boat

The lone swan spreads its wings: a fan
Blows in the cool of Mercy, the tent's
edges curl into rainclouds, out span
feathers, the river-swell portends
desire for the other shore, and drops
of rain turn parched soil into fields
of bread. Birds reap unsown seeds
incense-rings rise from ovens as manna

on the refugee's plate a fish-net crops
up, the boat lilts in waves of Hosanna
From across the shore come hymnal echoes—
Redeemed is the tent of fallen angels.

K. SATCHIDANANDAN

is a leading Indian poet. He is also perhaps the most translated of contemporary Indian poets, with thirty-two collections of translation in nineteen languages, including Arabic, Chinese, Japanese, English, Irish, French, German and Italian, besides all the major Indian languages. He has authored twenty-four collections of poetry, four books of travel, a full-length play and a collection of one-act plays, two books for children and several collections of critical essays, including five books in English on Indian literature, besides several collections of world poetry in translation. He has been a professor of English, and also the chief executive of the Sahitya Akademi, director of the School of Translation Studies, Indira Gandhi Open University, Delhi, and national fellow, Indian Institute of Advanced Study, Shimla. He is a fellow of the Kerala Sahitya Akademi and has won fifty-two literary awards from different states and countries, including the Sahitya Akademi Award, India-Poland Friendship Medal from the Government of Poland, knighthood from the Government of Italy and World Prize for Poetry for Peace from the Government of the UAE.

ON THIS EARTH*

1

We landed on earth from different stars
That is why we speak different languages.
Each word carries the aura
Of the memories of the stars we left.
In sleep we travel to those glittering homes.
There we speak to our forefathers
Like geckos that know
Every one of its walls.

We wake up to discover its stardust
On our skins.

2

From which star did you come?
I ask, watching the blue dust
On her shoulders at dawn.
She stares jealous at the red dust
On my chest.

We are now characters
in some science fiction
Even our heads do not look human.

3

As we die we return to the
Stars we left.
We will forget our sojourn on earth.
We will float in space,
As weightless souls, until we get
Another body and another language.

** Translated from the Malayalam by the poet.*

4

I want to be reborn on earth,
This time as a tree.
You will be a bird
perched on its bough.
I will recognize you by the
Blue dust on your wings.
And you, me with the
Red dust on my bark.

This time we won't quarrel.
I'll exchange my fruits for your song.
There won't be humans
To see or hear it.
Butterflies,
Only butterflies.

THE CIRCLE*

Joy is a narrow space
between two sorrows:
a space lit by the morning sun
where a sunflower is in bloom
amidst fresh blades of grass,
that two people can hardly occupy,
and may be a pale butterfly too.

You can dance there with
movements and gestures
possible in that narrow space.

---

* *Translated from the Malayalam by the poet.*

And sing in a low voice.
Can even laugh mildly
tickling the baby-sunlight.

But there is little time.
You know it too.
The sun will soon grow harsh.
Sorrows will squeeze you from both sides.
You may even get trapped there
never able to get out.

When the whole body bleeds,
you may suspect that joy is but a snare.
It is not all wrong, but you were able
to see the flower, and dance.

But pain—it is eternal,
and its space, infinite.
like the abyss that once trapped the earth.

You will have to leave the earth
to see there are stars even there.
Who knows, your soul
may fly across many lightyears
to land in a star.

It will gain a new body there.
Then you will know,
joy is but a narrow space
between two sorrows.

THE TRAIN*

(Remembering the stranded migrant workers of India)

That train is going to my village;
But I am not in it
Its rails are inside me
Its wheels are on my chest
And its whistle is my scream.

I won't be there
When it comes back to take me
But my breath will travel
Seated on its roof,
Guarding my corpse.

As the train stops at my village,
My life will enter my body
And ride my waiting bicycle
Along the old familiar lanes.
My children will come running
As they hear its bell:
'Abbu is here! Abbu is here!'

In which language can I tell them
It is my dead body that has arrived?
Of heaven, or of hell?
I am somewhere in between.

Let the well talk, or the pond.
If water refuses to speak
Let my life dwell within a crow
On the drumstick tree on my courtyard
And tell them the truth.

Translated from the Malayalam by the poet.

SUDEEP SEN

is a well-known Indian poet. His prize-winning books include *Postmarked India: New & Selected Poems* (HarperCollins), *Rain, Aria* (A.K. Ramanujan Translation Award), *Fractals: New & Selected Poems | Translations 1980-2015* (London Magazine Editions), *EroText* (Vintage: Penguin Random House), and *Kaifi Azmi: Poems | Nazms* (Bloomsbury). He has edited influential anthologies, including *The HarperCollins Book of English Poetry, World English Poetry* and *Modern English Poetry by Younger Indians* (Sahitya Akademi). For more on him, log on to www.sudeepsen.org.

HOPE: LIGHT LEAKS

'Darkness cannot drive out darkness.
Only light can do that.'
—Martin Luther King, Jr.

Late at night, light leaks—spilling
beyond the door's rectangle edge—

a cleaving schism, its shape—
a partial crucifix, a new resurrection.

Light's plane waxes, wanes—
viral load expands, contracts.

Photons spill, conduction sparks—
light slow removes cataract's veil.

In this *blackness, lives matter.*

SPEAKING IN SILENCE

(for Fiona)

Breathtaking weather surrounds us in these dark times.
I find calm in *Come Down*—misreading your book

title as 'calm down'—as if I am seeking balance for us
and others we love. Island climate can be promiscuous.

Indian songbirds outside my study tweet, pigs on
your English downs grunt—texting a common tongue.

come down / as everything breaks off / mid-story . . .
tractor tracks / a bucket at a gate / traces of the ones
who left just this morning / centuries ago

It was centuries ago, yet I know this place well—
we have walked together in this slurry and squelch.

In the coppice, I picked a driftwood piece—
sculpt-etched by wind-water—a Palaeolithic

talisman I left on your rustic kitchen window. Perhaps
it lies there still—exactly there, on the sunlit sill.

and water shakes / old terrors / loose . . . you could take /
this with you / your whole life || now everything / begins
to move / and everything stays / where it is

We speak in poetic phrases, punctuated by dactyls
and trochees, inundating line-breaks with half-rhymes—

this is the only language left, our private renga—
ancient codes dictating our syntax, not our accent.

As the world pandemically wrestles with dry heat
of disease and pestilence—profiteers pry, pilfer.

dry season / in the heart / you have to pray /
although you can't / but still the valves /
of the magnolia / wrench / themselves upward

Marigold-magnolia will bloom, nature will dance
perennially—fine-tuned in its horror and beauty.

It is we who do not heed its signs, understand
its corpuscle-conduct. We have long lived in lockdown—

'social distance' in solitary silos—mutating metaphors
spilling everywhere, defying state and statelessness.

flowers crowd / out of branches / that are holding / dark air up /
everything is / and knows it is—/ wild equinox ||
everything to come / hides its face / among the shaking tongues

I am certain we will continue walking, together and alone,
now and in the life-after—one's only guaranteed a lifetime

at most. Our silent speech stretches—like white,
its colours radiating beyond its spectrum-bandwidth,

beyond its infrared-ultraviolet—beyond infinite frequencies.
Whether it is chakra's sacred science, or just human belief—

time folds / into another century / where you come walking /
down with them / into the future / they won't arrive at ||
such a tender rite / it is that brings us home / to the light

that vanishes / and returns. Shall we return to aleph's source,
to oxhead's hieroglyph, to fountainhead's genesis—

to *a child / on a rope swing?* Are we on a robotic treadmill,
on a journey mapped out for us? Do we script our destiny

unlike nature's rolling hill-rains, unlike heat-dust-pestilence?
For now, let us *come down* for calm—to pause, reflect, love.

you were always here / in the body's / forethought
in its heft // heat and juice / in the smile /
of a stranger / who will never / speak your name

OBITUARY

'They were not simply names on a list.
They were us.'
—The New York Times

Death knells peal, numbers multiply,
virus ravages us, one by one.

Newspaper columns loom, unsteady
ghostly apparitions on broadsheets—

name, age, date of death—
tall epitaphs in fine print.

Ink spills, bleeds dark—newsprint
Blotting out our wheezing breath.

No amount of hygiene-ritual
enables our lungs to resuscitate.

Our lives—micro point-size fonts
on an ever-inflating pandemic list—

black specks, fugitive lonely numbers—
the deceased, on an official roster.

Another sick, another dying,
another dead—yes, *they were us.*

VIJAY SESHADRI

is the author of five collections of poems: *Wild Kingdom, The Long Meadow, The Disappearances, 3 Sections* and *That Was Now, This Is Then*; and several essays, reviews and memoir fragments. His work has been recognized with a number of honours, including the Pulitzer Prize for poetry. He teaches at Sarah Lawrence College.

PLAGUE THOUGHTS ENTER THE NEXT PHASE

'I just don't want to talk about it'

OK OK let's not

Not the stories the unbearable stories
You have five you don't want any more
You have fifteen how did you get so many

Because you live here
Because you *identify* here
Why do you live here why do you live anywhere
Identify anywhere

Because of all these
These the people
These the mysterious people
The people

Run run, says the plague
Some run out some run in some can't run
All are comprehended by the plague

Such a beautiful comprehender
Such a beautiful talker

Eloquent intelligent lucid precise
Analytical
Graphs charts little and big dots across the world
Such a teacher

About ourselves we are
Learning so much from you.

VARSHA SARAIYA-SHAH

is an Indian-American poet settled in the US. Her chapbook, *Voices*, was published by Finishing Line Press. Her poems have appeared in various journals and anthologies, including *Borderlands, Cha, Convergence, Echoes of the Cordillera, Mutabilis Press, Right Hand Pointing, Skylark UK, Soundings East, Texas Poetry Calendar*, and *UT Press Poetry & Photography*. Her work has featured on local public radio and been staged in a multi-language dance programme, *Poetry in Motion*, by Silambam, Houston.

I SPEAK FROM TOWERS OF SILENCE

It is spring, people are afraid
to sit on empty benches in parks
self-distancing. Coffin's length apart,
no matter where on the street or at work
dreading a footloose and lethal microbe.

Hugs are hats hung at the back door.
Babies like flowers can't stop being born,
mamas in hazmat suits swollen with milk
weep for their misfortune.

Imagine a massing of crows on terrace
gathered for feast to appease the dead.
Vultures plucking at corpses
I wish not to pollute air or water,
earth or fire. Let birds of prey feed on us.

Fire, Good fire, that burns to cleanse us all
of hunger and passion, anger and emptiness.
Assure the earth, it makes us part of our dirt.
Tell the skies, merge in your stardust.

O Invisible! Can you hear our dirge?
Italians belting out operas alone?
Tarantellas on balconies?
Hear the Spaniards banging pots,
strumming guitars in night skies?
Indians trumpeting conchs, chanting
Aum, Aum, Aum.

ADITYA SHANKAR

is a bilingual poet, flash-fiction author and translator. His poems have appeared in various journals worldwide and have been translated into Arabic and Malayalam. His poetry collections include *After Seeing* (2006), *Party Poopers* (2014) and *XXL* (2018). He has edited *Tiny Judges Shall Arrive* (AHRC, Hong Kong/Dhauli Books, India, forthcoming), a selection of K.G. Sankara Pillai's poems translated into English. *A Postcard to Voice* (forthcoming, Dhauli Books) is an anthology of his translation project, Malayalam Poetry in Translation, that was published in *Modern Literature*. His short films have participated in International Film Festivals. He lives in Bengaluru, India.

TOUCH

At times I feel
the best touch is a handshake.
A tree and a nest on it,
at liberty to be themselves.
The best touch is a rub of shoulders.
Strangers in adjacent train seats or
adjacent plots in a housing colony,
at ease in their silent camaraderie.
The best touch is the touch of wisdom
as you read lines that define you.
A pat on the back,
the blessing of mankind translated into a touch.
The touch of a smile,
a crescent moon that rose only for you.
The healing touch of hope.
The dreamy touch of winter in orchards.
The goodbye touch of eyes from the gallows.
The best touch is the hug of a father,
a private cartography of care.
The warmth of a mother,
the touch that you wish to hold forever.
The touch of love,
just how rain completes a crater.
The best touch is the hand of God.*
The saintly touch of Mother Teresa
on the sorrows of Kolkata.
The defining touch of Gandhi on the Indian soul.
Sorry, I'm not able to choose.
I'm composed of all the touches
that you planted on me.

---

*Hand of God: The goal scored by Diego Maradona, 1986 Football World Cup.

RAVI SHANKAR

is a Pushcart Prize–winning poet, translator and professor. He has published and edited over fifteen books, including the Muse India award-winning translations of ninth-century Tamil poet/saint, Andal, *The Autobiography of a Goddess* (Zubaan/University of Chicago), *The Golden Shovel: New Poems Honoring Gwendolyn Brooks* (University of Arkansas) and *The Many Uses of Mint: New and Selected Poems 1997-2017* (Recent Works Press). He has co-edited W.W. Norton's *Language for a New Century: Contemporary Poetry from the Middle East, Asia & Beyond*. He has founded one of the world's oldest electronic journals of the arts, *Drunken Boat*. Most recently, his collaborative chapbook, *A Field Guide to Southern China*, written with T.S. Eliot Prize winner George Szirtes, was published in the UK by Eyewear Publishing. His memoir, *Correctional*, is forthcoming in 2021.

LATIN FOR LIFE

A migraine so jasmine that it clings to the cortex
like a floor-length drape that obscures any view
from the window. Copley Square shines barren

of the unmasked, and even they are scant, dispersed
among the traces of spring which begin invisibly,
in the damp smell of earth and the tentative buds

of silver maples. Am I getting sick? Are you well?
A virus inhabits the grey zone between the animate
and inanimate, spreads unseen from touch, breath,

the very qualities that make us human. 'Staying
at home isn't a personal choice. It's an ethical duty,'
urges a retweeted headline while I eat my yogurt.

It's also the purview of the privileged, those of us
who can Zoom from home and still collect a paycheque.
The woman who bagged my groceries, Guatemalan,

is dead. I just read about her in *The Boston Globe*
and recognize her by her half-smile, by her fingers.
Vitalina Williams was her name and she's survived

by a husband who could not get close enough to her
in the hospital to say goodbye. He tells the reporter,
'Nobody's to blame, and everybody's to blame.'

She wasn't given a mask, because there weren't any.
The man who unloaded pallets of dairy products
from the back of a tractor trailer might be getting

sick and the migrant workers who work on farms
might be exposing themselves to deadly pathogens
so that we can all stay safe. That's democracy now.

That's the line between the haves and the have-nots.
There's a metaphor here, I think, hating myself
for thinking figuratively in the face of literal work.

How a virus attaches to a host cell, then penetrates
to replicate itself until it bursts from the membrane,
killing its host. It's stunning to see under the eye

of an electron microscope, aesthetically pleasing
even, a haloed Helen Frankenthaler abstraction,
although all I can see in mid-morning's throbbing

light is Vitalina's dark eyes and her brown fingers,
meticulously sorting the pasta sauce into one bag
and the eggs into another so that they won't break.

RA
SH

or Ravi Shanker N. has published three collections of poetry, *Architecture of Flesh* (Poetrywala, Mumbai), *The Bullet Train and Other Loaded Poems* (Hawakal Prokashan, Kolkata) and *Kintsugi by Hadni* (RLFPA Editions, Kolkata). He has also published individual poems in many national and international, online and print magazines. His poems have been translated into German and French. His collection of translated stories from Tamil, *Ichi Tree Monkey and Other Stories* (Speaking Tiger, Delhi), and a play, *Blind Men Write* (Rubric Publications, Delhi), are in the pipeline.

THE MALADY OF LOVE AND ITS REMEDY

Welcome to the Anti Love Virus Multi Specialty hospital
treating love and cloned simulations of it.

As the Hospital PRO, let me bluntly inform your dear selves
that Love is an infectious disease spread by a Virus that
entered earth's stratosphere with a falling asteroid that killed
many species. Love, therefore, is medically treated as an
inherently undesirable condition in any human.

Now, look at this state of the art machine that identifies the
presence of any form of the Love virus by
Myopic Heliographic Hyacynthixian Corrulo Resonance System.

The machine not only identifies and locates the Virus but also
issues veiled threats to it to leave the system.

Most viruses would prefer to evacuate following the Geneva
Convention Rule No 0.00.000.001.0001.

Those who don't agree are removed through surgical strikes.
Those that still don't perish are tortured every day in public
in a specially designed semi-transparent hydro tube of heat
sensitive
Krotium Collodium alloy that can heat the virus from Minus 2
K to K plus in one minute flat
thus eradicating it forever
with no chance of reincarnation.

This is a spectacular show of rainbow colours much loved
by the loving couples in the audience who hold hands with
surgical gloves and kiss through the surgical masks
their disinfected hearts wrapped in surgical gauze.

DEATH SHOWS ME SNOW

When death came for me,
I asked *him* to carry me
    (*him,* not *her,* death isn't a female)
through snow, not fire.

Have you never seen snow?
he asked [with pity]
I said, 'Have seen ice on sticks,
    in cups, as slabs, hailstorms,
    cubes, nuts, and as frozen fisheyes.
    never snow.'

So, death passed me
through a glass tube to where it snowed always
all my beloved ones watched me—
I travelled in style through glassy snow

I realized that snow was just frozen sperms;
    they broke through frozen ova and formed
    frozen zygotes till the tube warmed up
    heated to impossible temperatures
    akin to several suns

When the tube-ride ended,
we were thrown into a viscous ocean
that rumbled and yawned in
        the pangs of creation.

When I woke up in the hospital bed,
I was surrounded by evolving creatures—
        they sweetly sang a requiem for me, so sweet
    that my eyes brimmed over with distilled remorse

I asked them who they were,
they cried in unison,
'Death!'

LOVE IN THE TIME OF THE KARUNA* VIRUS

No one bothered till the Karuna virus caught the police
chanting the Hindu god's name and chasing Muhammedans
along with the mobs. The virus had its miraculous debut in
Shaheen Bagh when one by one the policemen stopped in
their tracks
and lowered the batons. The ones demolishing the mosques
stopped work
and came down as if nothing ever happened.

Some army men, who went back to Kashmir, carried the virus
with them and the torture camps were suddenly abandoned.
The army returned to the bases. Schools reopened. Internet was
restored in full. Streets were filled with singing dancing people.

The spread of the Karuna virus was swift. It swept across
Assam and the North
East. The detention camps were evacuated and people
streamed out in joy.

The virus entered China and the Uyghur Muslims were sent
back to families
from the concentration camps. Pro-democracy protesters were
let out of jail.
Same good news awaited the Rohingyas in Myanmar.

---

*Karuna means compassion.

North Korea ended their sham communism. By the banks of the Amazon forests,
the indigenous people were returned the forests. The wall between Mexico
and the US was demolished. US brought back all its marines from
Syria, Iraq and Afghanistan. Saudi Arabia banned capital punishment.
In Iran, the dissenters were released. Aboriginal rights were accepted in Australia.
The natives got their dues in the US. Israeli troops withdrew from Palestine.
All passports and visa restrictions were rendered invalid globally.

The symptoms of the Karuna virus were noticeable everywhere. People
were happy. Unburdened by wars, the governments spent more on food
and culture.

Happy couples roamed the streets in the cities and the villages freely, no one bothered them.

Me and my beloved entered the bamboo groves in the Western Ghats
and lay on the ground making love to the rhythm of the creaking trunks.
A snake slithered past our bodies. A bird pecked kindly at her nipples. Ants scurried along
my spine. A hundred fireflies lit up our dance of love.

A rain of Karuna fell upon us.

YUYUTSU SHARMA

is an Indian/Nepali poet and translator. He has published ten poetry collections, including *The Second Buddha Walk*, *A Blizzard in My Bones: New York Poems*, *Quaking Cantos: Nepal Earthquake Poems*, *Nepal Trilogy*, *Space Cake*, *Amsterdam* and *Annapurna Poems*. His work has been translated into German, French, Italian, Slovenian, Hebrew, Spanish and Dutch. He has also published a work of non-fiction, *Annapurnas & Stains of Blood: Life, Travel and Writing a Page of Snow* (Nirala, 2010).

RUNNING OUT OF INK

Running out of ink
like my karma to pen down

my grief as death rages
in the dank vaults of the world

and poison is sprinkled
with glee on my people

trapped in dog cages, beaten,
broken like stones in enclosed spaces

of hatred, abused and maimed
as their children cry out,

gasping for breath,
their journeys to reach distant homes

thwarted, mocked at,
their efforts to survive declared

uncouth and unconstitutional
by well-fed anchors sitting

on plush sofas
in the studios of current anarchy.

His giant potter's wheel plops out
piles of corpses, rightful relics of a wrath.

In my dream last night
I saw a blue Mediterranean shore crop up

in my backyard, a sudden sight
of joy at this grim hour.

From my rooftop
I see crystal waves crashing against mossy walls

of my ancestral house in Punjab
where once wheat fields stretched

to the rim of summer songs
of wailing hoopoes.

Life multiplies here in my village
even nails of the corpses flung into

the bottomless water wells
a decade before my birth

grow non-stop along with their black
shiny hair, eyelashes and long lush beards.

'Their women were so beautiful,
kohl-eyed, fair and sharp featured, houris,'

my grandma once
confided in my childhood,

'Death,' she said, 'is a discarded broom
of gloom, a misshapen, pygmy slur.'

The Queen mother in her tales cried so much
when the father of my hero, the king, brought in another wife

that she lost her eyesight
from crying all the time.

And Grandpa whispered the anecdotes
of his darker times when the British ruled.

The floods swamped the entire district,
everyone waded knee-deep in the muddy waters

and corpses of the animals
came floating to our doors, instead of singing saints.

On the seventh day he slept
in the main baithak of our house,

uttering prayers as the waters kept rising
ready to cross over our threshold

and the thunder roared
overhead all night long.

In the early hours of the dawn
he dreamt the waters rushing back

to the colossal mouth of the blue-throated god,
and life resuming its normal pace.

He woke out of his creaking cot
moved out of the house to step on the ground

dry as the bones
of our ancestral spirits.

MANOHAR SHETTY

is a poet and fiction writer who lives in Goa, India. He has eight books of poems to his credit, including *Full Disclosure: New and Collected Poems*, and is considered one of the prominent Indian poets. He has been a senior fellow with the Sahitya Akademi. Shetty's work has been published in several anthologies, including *The Oxford India Anthology of Twelve Modern Indian Poets*. He has edited *Ferry Crossing: Short Stories from Goa* and *Goa Travels: Being the Accounts of Travellers from the 16th to the 21st Century*. He is currently a Raza Foundation Fellow.

CORONA SONNETS

1

Just another fanciful name
For a virus to soften the blow
As they do with hurricanes—
Bhola or Katrina—and little to do
With the life-sustaining
Glow of the sun. It germinates
And breeds with the lightest
Touch or breath, leaving in its wake
Mass graves, quick cremations, the wheels
Of industry rusted, ore-rich mines
Caving in, exhaust pipes smokeless,
An exodus back to native
Villages and fields, the air
So pure you can barely breathe.

2

They can't sleep out on a park bench,
The terrace or backyard but are
Crammed into their hutments
Drenched with the sweat of cousins,
Parents, siblings, infants, distant
Relatives and frayed pictures
Of benign gods and goddesses.
The nation at a standstill, the long
March home is the only road open
To them even if their roots have grown
Fallow, even if their villages
Are shuttered like ghost towns, those
Silent raptors circling above.

LOCKDOWN SONG

Forced indoors, the mirror is your god.
It's time for personal grooming—manicures,
Pedicures and finicky facials
Though no one else is looking.

It's time to go on a diet and fitness regime
Though there's stuff, tinned and frozen,
Stowed away in your basement.
But in time you'll get heavier in body and mind.

For us garrulous folk across all ages
It's panic stations and a safe distance even
As millions feed off miracles in cow urine
And in the disembodied waters of the Ganges.

For the recluse, ascetic and jailbird it's nothing new.
The contagion, most democratic,
Knows no cure and can spread with just
One breath from patient to physician.

Out in slums and open roads
Their lungs are dustbins, the masks porous.
The cops rain down with their truncheons,
Imposing penance with frog-jumps.

Now the peacock, leopard and gazelle
Strut, prowl and leap across pavements.
They've reclaimed their space
As you stare down from your cage.

Now the long knives, edgy sickles,
And those native pistols hidden behind
Prayer books and idols of unforgiving gods
Are cocked and loaded.

Soon, from a mob they'll line up
In disciplined rank and file.
They'll defy the eternal curfew.
They have you, you and you in their sights.

THE NEW UNTOUCHABLES

The days tick past in slow motion,
The times not ripe for hugs and kisses,
For backslapping celebrations.

The deserted streets are like
A war zone though no sirens
Signal the all-clear, the enemy

Invisible or Novel. Magnified, it's akin
To an eerie spiky fruit, its venom
In touching distance with the labouring class

Now straggling, starving refugees.
It infiltrates posh apartments,
Movie stars and the richest nations.

For some, masks are a fashion statement
Even as that bereft woman
Gives birth under a roadside tree,

Even as the poor on the long march home
Need water to drink,
Not to sanitize their hands.

The malaise is not the usual
Rat or fly but it's said those vampire
Bats that go for the kill.

It has left the experts puzzled.

It has made us all guinea pigs.

It has made us the new untouchables.

H.S.
SHIVAPRAKASH

is an Indian poet and playwright writing in Kannada. He was professor at the School of Arts and Aesthetics, Jawaharlal Nehru University, New Delhi. He headed the cultural centre at Berlin, known as the Tagore Centre, run by the Indian Council for Cultural Relations (ICCR). He has seven anthologies of poems, twelve plays and several other books to his credit. Shivaprakash is also a well-known authority on *vachana* literature, Bhakti movements of India, and Sufi and other mystic traditions.

THE TOUCH

Let me touch you today
And also you, you and anyone
Without touching you
How sunlight touches the garden
Without touching it
How the stars touch each other
Without touching
How songs play in ears
Without touching them
How compassion touches the heart
Without touching it
We've touched too much between us
We have been too infected among ourselves
We enjoyed ourselves too much
No feelings
Getting sick among us
Every time we touch
getting too much joy
without giving it

Let us play today
Touch each other
Without touching
Just giving
Without possessing
Just delivering

The distance is now deleted
Even if you are close
I'm far here on an ocean shore
You are faraway on another
So far we can't touch each other with our hands

Only with our hearts
We can even see each other
Clearly from any distance
We can hear us
Without rushing to talk

Even our breathing
It's in tune
When the hearts touch
When souls touch each other

Until hands learn the lesson
They have forgotten for centuries
Until they remember why they started
To touch

Let them be hungry for touch
Until they learn again
To touch with the heart
To touch with the soul

How the guru touches the apprentice
In samadhi
How the ancestors touch us
In a vision
How the words of a dead poet
Touch the living

WHEN THE POET WENT TO SLEEP

When the poet went to sleep
She woke up in the dream world
Where stars were swimming
Like tiny fish in her river

She could turn the sun and the moon at will
Like a child can play with the wheels
Of a toy cart
Where she could cut, delete, correct or rewrite altogether
her past
Like on her laptop
On the sun's screen
Reflected in her lake of the heart
The present stood like a loyal maid
Waiting eagerly for her slightest command
And future was calling her on the mobile
To ask in what costumes she could come for her audience
She heard sometimes in whispers
Sometime rolling like a thunder
All her forgotten lines
While lightning inscribed
On the horizon
Lines she would write a whole age later
She found at her feet
In her magic garden a tiny yellow flower
Its centre opened out
Into another constellation
With a hundred more suns
Surrounded by earths more glorious than ours
On one of them she was pre-born
To see herself looking at this tiny flower
I watched all this happen in her dream
Like a still and silent hill
Watching the flow of seasons in the valley
Or formless space watching
The birth and death of mortal stars
And wrote it all down
On waking up

The poet had forgotten it all
When she saw this poem
I had calligraphed on her wall
Even then she remembered nothing
And thought it a wild fantasy
Of my making

NHLANHLA SILIGA

is a South African writer and poet. He is presently researching for his children's fantasy novel. He is also writing a Zulu drama book for children.

HANDYMAN

I was a handyman
Inside the walls of this lockdown.
I fixed my front door
that wouldn't let me in.
I fixed the bulb holder
that had refused to give me light
I fixed the broken stringless guitar
I found under the bed.
I fixed Spotty's kennel
In case I got a new dog.
I fixed the spelling errors
in all my poems
magazines had sent back.

On the last day
I called my ex-girlfriend
and told her:
Dear Parton, I apologize
for all the heartaches
I've caused you:
please forgive me.
Over the phone's receiver
I could hear her cry.
I forgive you, Nhlanhla, she said.

SAVITA SINGH

is a poet from Delhi. She writes in Hindi and English, and has three poetry collections to her name: *Apne Jaisa Jeevan*, *Neend Thi Aur Raat Thi* and *Swapna Samay*. A collection of her poems has been translated into French as *Je Suis La Maison Des Etoiles*. Her poetry has been translated into German, Spanish, Portuguese, Dutch and Catalonian. She is a recipient of the Hindi Academy Award, the Raza Foundation Award and the Mahadevi Varma Award. She works in the area of gender studies and has written on feminist theories of state, economy and literature. She is a professor in the School of Gender and Development Studies, at the Indira Gandhi National Open University, New Delhi.

DEATH, WHERE DO YOU DWELL?*

Where do you peep at us from, death? When the evening
steps out of her clothes, disrobes. When the night begins
to blink?

Actually, I don't really want to think of you now.
I'd rather ponder that eternal, that infinite.

She, who is interred, still turning lifelike
sadnesses, outside and within, into utter sameness.

Death, I command you! Disappear.

Really, where are those places you go on
marking your presences? Go there.

What did you just say? You occupy
every direction, expanse, every region, aeon.

How then, to recognize you?
Are you a germ, a bacteria, virus?
A train, a truck? A plane. Or are you
that bed, upon which people renounce their lives?

That zero-ness where the beloved disappear,
are you there? Who are you?

Though, like hunger, many have grown
to know you as one does hunger itself.

Yet what, and whose inanition are you?
That of love, consciousness, or simply, the gut's yearning?

How do you kill off a person, with this sort of hunger?

Do others also pet this variety of craving?
Don't ask me, no, to interrogate the lovers for an answer.

Translated from the Hindi by Medha Singh.

Show me the sonorous winds of your zeroes
Where that eight-year-old girl went

to be ganged up on, killed off in bed
in sleep, unconsciousness
in the place of God. Can you be seen?

Have we, us, confronted each other?
Do you resemble a woman in a veil?

What, after all, ever stays concealed
between you and this universe?
I could see into your eyes one day—
a buoying, infinitesimal creature.

A world of shadows floating in time.

All that seemed, wasn't what it seemed.
I'm stuck in this strange vagueness.

Is it possible to meet there?
To meet those we've lost.

The Asifa we lost?
Is she safely wrapped in herself, her body, over there?
Do our births, our memorials, loves, transforming
into betrayal, will they all, all be safe in themselves?

Our sins, cruelties, do you possess all of them
within your windy emptiness?

Is death really a kind of slumber? This life
a dream? I'm the one who says this first.

Yet somehow it feels like aged wisdom.
Are you often recognized, do you switch

disguises? Do you keep renewing

growing less certain, yet more heartless
with each duty you've carried out?

When will you approach me? Arriving
as a ship? I have a premonition

that I'll climb up a barque one day
and it shall take me with itself
as it drowns. Always afraid of water, I
grow dizzy on boats.

The vessel tearing through water,
never looking at its tip

Staring at the sky, I continue
until we are safely docked.

I love walking most.
You, you could knock me over as a bicycle,

and be on your way.

I wouldn't even feel it, dying an ordinary death
is what I'd like best.
No cannon salute for me,
I'd go without the slightest noise.

If there's one thing I'd not want, is to be lynched.
None to force a 'Jai Shri Ram!' out of me.
No officer causing my soil
to vanish. That when I go, I go

without making a mess, without
being quartered, eviscerated.

Go, the way a wind glides from a valley to another
a bird flitting from branch to branch.

ARI SITAS

is a South African poet, dramatist, social activist and sociologist. He has had an illustrious academic career and activist life. His poetic works include *Tropical Scars* (1989), *Songs, Shoeshine and Piano* (1991), *Slave Trades* (2000), *RDP Poems* (2004), *Around the World in 80 Days: The India Section* (2013), *Rough Music* (2014) and *Vespa Diaries* (2018). *Oratorio* is being published by Tulika Press and Columbia University Press in 2020.

LOCKDOWN

Like shaving cream, a bowl of cream soft on the cheek, a
razor hard on the cheek, stuff to shave with in the early-
morning breeze, my ears flapping, flapping ears, each
thing a single commodity, a mere purchase, each one
alongside others, tons of others, immense accumulation of
others, pure wealth.
In my private theatre: there has to be an inevitable crossing/has
to be bleak, has to have the desert as its furthest stretch.
Umuzi ngumuzi ngokuphanjukelwa
The passing too, the passing is not a passing ngokuphanjukelwa
That is not the spiritual side that I intended by getting up
this brand-new morning, I can make a sign of the cross
to confuse my ancestors and bless our brand-new day
and admire at the distance the melancholy mountain, the
Vodacom towers like stiff exotic palm trees. And there,
unanointed by me and irritable at my rapid crosses and the
chanting of a Good Friday hymn before the cavalry attacks
the landscape stands unmoved—the cavalry charge—a wall
of neighing horseheads.
No, the crossing—it has to beckon me in to walk through or
walk by or walk right in/there have to be birds, thirsty
birds atop the sun-licked bone of camel heads
Anti-Icarus: the closer to the sun, the colder it gets
I read that the cell phone went to market to find money.
Money went to market to find a cell phone. Supply the
demand and demand the supply, quite balanced. The
church bell was on automatic timer, a dolphin complied
far out on the third ring to cackle and dive.
There was a Zoom meeting.
The Zoom meeting is not a zoom meeting, ngokuphanjukelwa
There have to be tree trunks, sunk tree trunks, branches akimbo,
withered, warped sunk into the sides of imposing sand dunes

The sun never sets

If you listen carefully someone is still digging for gold. But the gold bosses left on pre-Covid wings their quarters now stand in ruin, someone threw something hard through the glass and auctioned the plaster, the mortar, but the bricks stand firm, the lockdown has locked down the folk—bereft, no one left to hurl them. A riot in my mind . . . brickless.

There have to be indignant sand dunes, surfaces have to be taut for the wind to drum a hapless cross-rhythm

It is not the stars that lose their way

The cell phone was not alone of course, of course, there were other things, solid and ephemeral circling, circling but the money was quite the same, being encircled whilst circling, making up eddies apparently all the way to Vanaatu and back to the Easter islands, is your cough dry or liquid, does it have the rattle of a snake as phlegm gathers to bounce out with your lung puff to wow . . . is this a dance of sorts, don't the rocks in the path hurt the soles of your feet, or are they not rocks but just abandoned coins? Was your cough dry or liquid?

There has to be a boat beached against the dune's side, torn sail chirring and a sound of a seagull somewhere . . . surely

There is this dervish dance, Sufi-foxtrot perhaps, as the money turns to what Marx called capital or was it Ricardo or the other Chinese chap who after they did sail to Patagonia and Malindi didn't they and gathered metaphors and samples, but they were only interested in silver and silver can be confused for gold in bright sunlight, like even the spawn from the sea turns golden at the right time, and gold turns bluish at dusk, but unlike all other metals, who turn rust green, not the verdant green but the mucus-like green that you get off the nostril of a wandering hippo, gold never rusts. I can hear someone digging.

Our dancing often disturbs the anthill
There has to be an ocean somewhere, there has to be an
inevitable crossing.
The philosopher in us wants to understand how come, money
does not turn into capital by itself, why in the act of
enveloping a thing as price, it remains as price spent and
nothing else, a memory, a discarded piece of toe jam or a
song your mother sung to you as if that could deal with
fever, puff gone and the dentures you just purchased,
used because no one can afford a new one, even in the
here where it is not America, and there the silent ship
coming to harbour could be full of these used ones from
somewhere East.
There is poverty:
The cat sleeps on the cold embers
Umuzi ngumuzi ngokuphanjukelwa

FROM HOODING

Uprooting baobab trees
to dig up coal was the first moment
and then being put on carbon diet was the second—

we had excuses you know, there were men with guns
and we felt sorry for the clean-up workers
and our eyes were gouged out, we couldn't see
the world was opaque,
and
at least we missed the celebrations of how
they
saved the nation and received bonuses and medals

and how a handful of bankers nursed all of our ills
they said we disappeared
we said we were disappeared
but facts are facts, the drones spotted us leaving

ok there was a little nod here and there and a . . . don't breathe
a word

out
to anyone, be wary of carpenters, tanners and women that
weave
boxes and shrouds and as you also know flayed skin is always a
bad omen
pick up some sour plums from the neighbour's orchard and
line up
line up
so . . . we left
herding men, herding animals
with a blind man leading our procession
and many of us feigning blindness we marched far
until our feet were bleeding
come on poet, speak it, as Dylan said, don't blow it
even if we marched through the cool
of verdant forests

the blind man leading was wondrous
but I want my blindness to be different:
I want to confess to a hood
and underneath, the poet's eye:
pure peregrine falcon!

RAFAEL SOLER

is a major Spanish poet and an award-winning novelist. He is a professor and the vice-president of the Spanish Writers' Association. He has published five books of poetry in Spanish. He has won the Juan Ramon Jimenez Prize (1980) and the Critica Valenciana Prize (2016). Soler has been invited to read poetry in more than fifteen countries. Two of his collections have been published in South America and his books have been translated into English, French, Italian, Japanese, Hungarian and Romanian.

WHAT I REQUEST HAS A NAME*

May the last one to die not remain
in order to please us
dressed in mourning from head to toe
and his gaze fixed on a silence
that even the rain ignores

May the poor thing go with the buddies
also precociously dark
their souls on the verge of shipwreck
and their shoes dirty

May they by threes towards the clouds depart
and in a foggy doorway search for their stairway
taking possession of everything they are lacking
including as they say
the resurrection of the flesh
the forgiveness of sins
and eternal life anyway.

** Translated from the Spanish by Gwendolyn Osterwald.*

NO PRICE IS TOO HIGH*

If your life doesn't fit into a lifetime
write a premature will

Organize the kisses that you wasted
and go back along the line that leads
to what is honourable about routine

Seek the chest where almost everything fits
and leave it behind in its meagre abundance

And may the life on the screen always be
the life in the movie seat that awaits you

** Translated from the Spanish by Gwendolyn Osterwald.*

CHRIS SONG

is a poet, translator and editor based in Hong Kong. He has published four collections of poetry and many volumes of poetry in translation. In 2018, he obtained a PhD in Translation Studies from Lingnan University. Song received an 'Extraordinary Mention' at Italy's UNESCO-recognized Nosside World Poetry Prize 2013. He is now executive director of the Hong Kong International Poetry Nights and editor-in-chief of *Voice & Verse Poetry Magazine*.

SONG OF DESPAIR IN THE TIME OF THE PANDEMIC

We share atypical memory
Some died obscured
We sing our grief; riot control echoes
Still purging tear smoke from the heart
we resigned ourselves to blood buns
The drugstore clerk rolls down the shutters
wearing a mask in the dark, his eyes glitter
dead set on the pneumonia
Some fall silent but fulfilled
Others speak but emptied

We choke on water and cough
Eyes doubt, bodies lean off
elbows panic, as indifferent as sensitive
The mask puffs with breathing
The number of cases grows every day
The sun sets to grill the officials
making efforts not to close the border
A breach remains forever closing
Some decide to go on strike
Others plan to settle scores

We draw a neutral stick in the temple
Spring drizzle muses on the growth of mould
Haven't worshipped door gods for many years
Let's have the ones auspicious for health
Stew a soup, get rid of the damp-heat
and cleanse the lung. Speaking of which,
Qingming is approaching, let's burn
some paper masks to replace the offerings
Some want to go out for a mask hunt
Others stay in unwilling to speak

Silhouettes show up on the cruise deck
and soon disappear into the mist
We wave ambiguous hands from the shore
How should we meet them after the mist lifts?
We cut short the travel and rush back for shelter
Capricious on the border is the body temperature
Contagious in Lan Kwai Fong are tear and laughter
Sober up, go to the gym, and get another round!
Some spread panic wearing a mask
So do others not wearing one

The fridge is stuffed with frozen dumplings
Can we regain the warmth of home?
Self-isolated in the small flat
the relatives we miss are always far-off
We follow a recipe to make a family dish
but still we lack the seasonings of lineage
Rationing affection and toilet paper
let's practice living the life in the apocalypse
Some roll deprived of sleep during the day
Others sneak out to line up for masks at daybreak

The corona iris stares down the world
A pandemic crystalizes the hostility of eyes
immune to the colour and tongue of hatred
The poet who pondered on virtue and justice
passed on. You and I continue to lyricize
Shadows of the virus bewilder our strokes
from the beginning of spring to the vernal equinox
The summer still seems far. Will I see you again?
An outcry bursts out of the lion rock
Earth and sky echo a whimper of despair.

SRIJATO

has established himself as one of the primary exponents of modern Bengali poetry. Srijato was also invited to attend the writer's workshop at Iowa State University (2006) and was the representative for Bengali poetry at the International Book Festival, Edinburgh, Scotland (2008), as well as at the prestigious Hay Festival, Wales (2017). Srijato's first book, *Sesh Chithi: The Last Letter*, was published in 1999. He is the author of more than twenty books of modern Bengali poetry. A collection of his poems, *Mushtaq Hussain's Darbari*, has been translated into English by Arunava Sinha. Srijato has received many awards, including the Ananda Puraskar, Krittibas Puraskar, Bangla Academy Puraskar as well as the Filmfare East Award for best lyricist.

MIRROR*

What sleep is this, where even you are not there?
The neighbourhood grows more desolate than dreams
Our identity shatters if no one is here
As mirrors lose value where no face brims.

For thousands of years, they have been walking in a league
Still none has had Jibanananda's fame
Singhal is gone, and Natore too is bleak
Those who are on the road, does ever home belong to them?

Which is this path, where even you are reticent
To a future, ancient, it leads
Awareness is but a joke, played by the moment
Plague, in its name, still rumour breeds.

We lived in love in this planet, content,
Bloodsheds require witness too,
The vessel floats off to the far-off continent,
And men walk, for years, they do . . .

Rather, let me see you more up close
The simple lines in your complex eyes
Even if you survive, will love? Those
Questions are learnt where defeat lies.

If we lose, we meet again no more
Why such haste in this departure
Stuck in the wall of a dead planet, forsaken
Valueless, without a face, as hangs the mirror.

---

* *Translated from the Bengali by Rohan Hassan.*

KIM STAFFORD

is an American poet and essayist who lives in Portland, Oregon. He holds a PhD in medieval literature from the University of Oregon. Since 1979, he has taught writing at Lewis & Clark College in Portland. He has also taught courses at Willamette University in Salem, at the Sitka Center for Art and Ecology, at the Fishtrap writers' gathering, and private workshops in Scotland, Italy and Bhutan. In July 2018, he was appointed Oregon's Poet Laureate.

CONVENT PRINT SHOP

After the pandemic, in the second spring,
when, at last, we all began to get about again,
the good Sisters, who had been sheltering in place
for a thousand years, began to hear, when children
came to help or be blessed, legends of ordinary
saints in hard times—the homeless man who carried
food to camps and buried the lost when no one came,
the mother who taught school to hundreds by Zoom,
mechanic who repaired the ambulance again and again,
girl who played her flute from the rooftop, singing
her soul for the housebound, farmer who delivered
produce boxes to anonymous curbs, nurse who
ministered when the doctor died.

They printed these as verses, stories, hymns and psalms,
like the little flowers of Francis and Clare, to give away
in all directions, as the plum trees burst into bloom.

BIRD HOUSE HAT

In quarantine, at last, I have
time to stand so still, all flit
and whir the wren comes
curious to try the twig perch,
peer through the knothole
in my contraption, balanced
tall and Eden-like, to find
in the hollow dark inviting
grass, moss, and thistledown
at ready for the weaving,

while I behind closed eyes
in tree pose, breathing
long and slow, await
the restoration.

SHELTER IN PLACE

Long before the pandemic, the trees
knew how to guard one place with
roots and shade. Moss found
how to hug a stone for life.
Every stream works out how
to move in place, staying home
even as it flows generously
outward, sending bounty far.
Now is our time to practise—
singing from balconies, sending
words of comfort by any courier,
kindling our lonesome generosity
to shine in all directions like stars.

ARUNDHATHI SUBRAMANIAM

is an acclaimed Indian poet. She is the author of five books of poetry, most recently *Love Without a Story* (Amazon Westland, New Delhi, 2019), and *When God Is a Traveller* (HarperCollins India, New Delhi, 2014, and Bloodaxe Books, Newcastle, 2014). Her prose books include *The Book of Buddha*, the bestselling biography of a contemporary mystic, *Sadhguru: More Than a Life*, and most recently, *Adiyogi: The Source of Yoga* (co-authored with Sadhguru). As editor, her most recent book is the Penguin anthology of sacred poetry, *Eating God*. She is the recipient of various awards and fellowships.

THE WORLD TAKES A BREATH

The world takes a breath

noisily—

recycling anodyne
text messages
about the wisdom
of looking within,

photographs of mute anguish
to give us our daily fix
of indignation,

a wild pandemic
of pieties.

Who'd have thought
an empty hour
was so much labour?

We walk the day most times
on steel girders
of habit

knowing that as long as there are lists
the world is safe,

and meaning won't save us
(never has),
but rhythms will.

And only sometimes
does all the fumbling
and twitching
swivel
into

immaculate choreography

and the sky falls away
like blue laughter

and suddenly, we're cycling,

hands free, hands free,

on air.

I'M LEARNING

I'm learning about breeze:

how at times it turns
lemony, weightless, eternal,

breathed by Dutch traders
in Tranquebar

and classical Tamil heroines,
sharp

and greenly spare
as Ramanujan pen strokes.

About irrelevance:

learning to stand
(on wobbly knees)
behind my breath.

About that cliché, time:

the way it shifts its weight
like a guilty schoolgirl

from one foot
to the other,

now paralysis,
now pure sunlit velocity.

And birds
(who isn't learning about birds?):

how their song subsides
when we speak of it.

But what of those days
when we even learn
consolation?

Not just because squirrels
are planning a family

outside this window,
but because the world

no longer neighs
and foams

in an old drama
of outrage and hoofdust,

but wakes
most mornings

looking simply
somewhat

puzzled.

THE NEWS

Learn something new every day,
say the wise ones

and so we try.

The news today
is that there's no one
at the Champs Élysées,

no one
at the Gateway of India,
no one at all
in the spice market of Istanbul,
the souk at Aleppo,

that the great theatres
and pulsating green rooms
of the world
lie plunged in darkness,

that pigeons hover
like suspended confetti
above the piazza of San Marco,

that no one's ordering
double macchiatos
in East Village cafés,

that a woman walking back
to her village from Telangana
died of starvation
in a Chhattisgarh forest.

Her news
(and it isn't particularly new)

is that we're always eleven miles
away from home.

COMMANDMENT

When the world channels Rumi
you don't get Rumi.
You get candyfloss.

GEORGE SZIRTES

was born in Hungary and emigrated to England with his parents—survivors of concentration and labour camps—after the 1956 Budapest uprising. His first book, *The Slant Door* (1979), won the Faber Memorial Prize. *Bridge Passages* (1991) was shortlisted for the Whitbread Poetry Prize. *Reel* (2004) won the T.S. Eliot Prize, and his *New and Collected Poems* was published by Bloodaxe in 2008. Szirtes has also written extensively for radio and is the author of more than a dozen plays, musicals, opera libretti and oratorios. He has translated, edited and anthologized numerous collections of Hungarian poetry. Szirtes has won several awards for his translation work, including the Dery Prize for Imre Madach's *The Tragedy of Man* (1989) and the European Poetry Translation Prize for Zsuzsa Rakovsky's *New Life* (1994). His own work has been translated into numerous languages and widely anthologized, including in Penguin's *British Poetry Since 1945*.

SMALLPOX

Science for the curious, is what it says
on the slick caption. The curious are pressed
tightly into a book, still hoping to be blessed.
Each bears a coffin at which someone prays.

Crosses, coffins and cowls determine them
according to the medieval scheme
of superstition, death and troubling dream.
It's half cosmology, half stratagem.

Do smell them, Highness, as they struggle on.
The plague exhausts them. Science moves off stage,
just one pale rider left and one bare field

to conjure with. And soon they are all gone.
There are no options here except to yield
or else keep hoping someone turns the page.

BLACK DEATH

The man with broad-brimmed hat and bird-mask waits
a moment before entering. His scent
wafts by you, Highness, as presentiment
of what must follow. Watch how he operates

in his full gown. Observe how he inspects
the body, turning it here and there at distance
with his cane, meeting no resistance.
Note how he prods it. He's the bird that pecks

at corruption. He sees the patient's hands
are black with the usual buboes. This is all

by the script. It's the very reason for his call.
The plague is spreading. It makes strict demands.

We watch familiar birds hovering in the air.
They will not ring the bell. Nor are we there.

CHOLERA

Everything begins somewhere. Everything is 'here'.
Here is where the enemy starts his long
arduous campaign, launching the first spear.
He has no home, has no desire to belong

to just one place and so he moves about.
Two skeletons clench by a fetid pool,
and soon a table with a glass of stout
and cloudy water carry one to stool

another to feast. You watch a man collapse
at one point on the map, one street, and soon
everyone's falling. Death runs from open taps
and drops from the singer's mouth. There are few
remaining, Highness. We watch the sun at noon
rise ever higher, burning off late dew.

SPANISH FLU

The khaki flu. The extra years of war
that is no war. From country seats to huts,
from shacks to palaces. You can't keep score
of numbers. State by state the country shuts

its eyes and mouth and soon begins to drown.
Its skin turns blue and within hours it's dead.
The rest wear masks and camphor. The whole town
is dream terrain, a dull street-plan of dread.

The cull is on, Your Highness. World is thinning.
Let's call it nature or divine constraint.
It is the way we've lived since the beginning.
Cover the doors in blood or chalk or paint.

That is the age-old troubled human scene.
It's time for better drugs and quarantine.

COVID-19

Now here we are in quarantine, our ears
sharpened to the footsteps stalking us.
We watch the passing of the empty bus
as one more phantom carrier appears

and swerves around us grinning as he goes.
Elsewhere the poor are jammed into their rooms
to gaze from blocks that reek too much of tombs
intended for them, while the virus throws

its net across the whole estate like smoke.
Observe, Highness, how some of them remain
still poorer, and while you and I should live,

survival will be harder to forgive,
though later it might serve for a black joke,
that you, Highness, might very well explain.

ADAM TAMASHASKY

teaches at American University, in Washington, D.C. His poetry has appeared in *Delmarva Review, The Cold Mountain Review, The Innisfree Poetry Journal* and *491 Magazine*. He grew up in Cincinnati, Ohio, and studied at the University of Dayton for his undergraduate degree and at American University for his MFA.

HOMECOMING

I will return the winding way
through the beleavèd forest's floor.

Through greened sunlight I'll slip and sluice,
living dew 'midst dying day's dusk.

I'll light upon leaves left lying
asleep athwart the sylvan silt,

no step noising, nor breath breaking,
nor quaver cracking quiescence.

Find me, friend, afore I arrive;
meet midway among the maples—
Hands a-twined let's homeward ramble.

ANITHA THAMPI

is a Malayalam poet. Her first poetry collection, *Muttamadikkumpol*, was published in 2004 to significant critical acclaim. Her other works include *Azhakillaathavayellam* (2010), *Alappuzha Vellam* (2016) and a trilingual co-authored collection, *A Different Water* (2018). She has translated works by several writers, including Juan Ramón Jiménez, Les Murray and Mourid Barghouti. She lives in Thiruvananthapuram, Kerala.

PASSAGES

A tiny bird tumbled down,
its wings struck against the sound
of my walking along the mind
of a passage without passers-by

A tree waiting for the sun
to dry its loose hair
stopped it from falling.

The sound of my laughter
formed a little lane in the mind
of the passage
without passers-by.

SHE WHO WEEPS

Who unrolls the world
to sleep on?
Who dusts
and spreads it out?

Who shoots hope
into this sky?
Who lies awake all night?

Let us ask the lame puppy
sleeping on the courtyard
of the thatched little cottage

The puppy gently
groans and limps.
Who is it that weeps and
waters this world?

NGUGI WA THIONG'O

is a celebrated Kenyan writer and academic who writes primarily in Gikuyu. His work includes novels, plays, short stories and essays, ranging from literary and social criticism to children's literature. He is the founder and editor of the Gikuyu-language journal *Mũtĩĩri*. His short story, 'The Upright Revolution: Or Why Humans Walk Upright', has been translated into more than ninety languages from around the world. In 1977, Ngugi embarked upon a novel form of theatre in his native Kenya that sought to liberate the theatrical process from what he held to be 'the general bourgeois education system', by encouraging spontaneity and audience participation in the performances. He taught at Yale University for some years, and also at New York University and at the University of California, where he is distinguished professor of English and Comparative Literature.

DAWN OF DARKNESS

I know, I know,
It threatens the common gestures of human bonding
The handshake,
The hug
The shoulders we give each other to cry on
The neighborliness we take for granted
So much that we often beat our breasts
Crowing about rugged individualism,
Disdaining nature, pissing poison on it even, while
Claiming that property has all the legal rights of personhood
Murmuring gratitude for our shares in the gods of capital.

Oh how now I wish I could write poetry in English,
Or in any and every language you speak
So I can share with you, words that
Wanjikũ, my Gĩkũyũ mother, used to tell me:
Gũtirĩ ũtukũ ũtakĩa:
No night is so Dark that,
It will not end in Dawn,
Or simply put,
Every night ends with dawn.
Gũtirĩ ũtukũ ũtakĩa.

This darkness too will pass away
We shall meet again and again
And talk about Darkness and Dawn
Sing and laugh maybe even hug
Nature and nurture locked in a green embrace
Celebrating every pulsation of a common being
Rediscovered and cherished for real
In the light of the Darkness and the new Dawn.

ASHOK VAJPEYI

is a Hindi poet, critic and a major cultural figure of India. Apart from more than fifteen books of poetry, ten of criticism in Hindi and four books on art in English to his credit, he has three books in English translation, one in French and two in Polish, besides in six Indian languages. Widely recognized as an outstanding promoter of culture and an innovative institution-builder, he has raised his voice for the autonomy of literature and the arts against contemporary tyrannies of ideologies, markets and fundamentalism. Vajpeyi has received several awards, including the Sahitya Akademi Award.

NO, WE WON'T BE ABLE TO WRITE OUR TIME*

This stilled and deserted time
where even birds and beasts are silent
where the daily noises have been
replaced by mere echoes,
where prayers, calls and cries have
alike dissolved in silence,
where friendships lie unexpressed
where silence is spread over everything like Time:

How do we write such time?
Don't know whether this is our time,
Or whether we have been forced
to enter another time
This time is so even that on it we see
no wrinkles, folds or holes
and we hardly find a passage to flee.
No, we won't be able to write our time.

This time is moving so slow that all clocks
Seem determined to go slow
The wind is cold before its season
The spring has just come and flowers blossom
As if to laugh at our evil times
And squirrels race irritatingly fast
and climb trees or pillars
Pigeons have suddenly grown less in number
As if they too have set on their sad trips back
to their village-homes like the migrant workers:
Even being in our homes seems a solace

**Translated from the Hindi by K. Satchidanandan.*

we are at least in our homes
if not in our times.

Hope is lying in some corner pressed down
like a piece come off some waste
that is sure to be swept off and thrown away
tomorrow if not today.
No, we won't be able to write our time.

FIVE SHORT POEMS*

1
The first bird of the morning cries
tearing to pieces the darkness that still remains,
but the morning does not know.

2
There are voices in solitude
There are no words, no people
And yet the dawn arrives on time

3
Birds have not said anything,
No one told them anything
The birds have silently brought the dawn
on their tiny wings.

4
Perhaps darkness knows it has to end
Perhaps light knows its time will come
Perhaps it is us humans who are stuck between
being and non-being

---

*Translated from the Hindi by K. Satchidanandan.

5

Some things just keep vanishing all the time
without our knowing it:
the first melodies and images of childhood,
the face of the man who silently lifts
the blanket in the train,
the well-known refrain of Lalit
one fails to recall in the morning,
the day last year when the Flame of the Forest
turned flamboyant with so many flowers . . .
Some things just keep vanishing all the time . . .

PRAMILA VENKATESWARAN

is Poet Laureate of Suffolk County, Long Island (2013-15), and co-director of Matwaala: South Asian Diaspora Poetry Festival. She is the author of *Thirtha* (Yuganta Press, 2002), *Behind Dark Waters* (Plain View Press, 2008), *Draw Me Inmost* (Stockport Flats, 2009), *Trace* (Finishing Line Press, 2011), *Thirteen Days to Let Go* (Aldrich Press, 2015), *Slow Ripening* (Local Gems, 2016) and *The Singer of Alleppey* (Shanti Arts, 2018). An award-winning poet, she teaches English and Women's Studies at Nassau Community College, New York.

VARIATIONS OF THE EERIE

I am the only car driving through the Queens Midtown Tunnel
into Manhattan. Am I inside a horror film? Streets sit vacant,
emptied of crowds, stores stay shut. Traffic lights grill
wet roads. But the city lies comatose, its eerie plight
a variation from the crazed nightmare unfolding in hospitals,
where gurneys bearing the dead are piled into freezers
in trucks, while the living sick wait like scared gulls:
for beds, then oxygen, then respirators.
We are between life and death, caught in the net
of 'the plague', which even now eats our lungs,
the delicate fabric of our breath. Doctors wrest
us from the brink, their expert care, their offerings.
But the demon demands more than human sacrifice.

CREDO OF THE LITERALIST

Termites eat a whole house.
A bug brings down an oak.
One person ousts a government.
A microbe upends a world.
We learn to stay alone.
The hours of a day fill up with sleep.
Cooking and eating rise into arts.
We write and rewrite dreams.
My email announces my friend's death.
My keening floods the yard.
We lose audiences.
No need to juggle priorities.
Sisyphus is frozen.
The cross means 'Cancelled'.

XABISO VILI

is an African performer, writer and social activist. His writings explore his inner world to relate to the outer world. He is the champion of multiple slams and poet of the year awards. Xabiso has been published in various anthologies and online. He has performed all over South Africa, in Scotland, the UK, the US and India.

THE NEW MIGRATION

Watch how the city empties itself,
drips migrating bodies, black,
out of its lungs,
its greying walls
no longer able to disguise
the faded gold
it promised to the fathers
of the children
who fill the national roads.
This place rolls them
in newspapers and bibles
and tars its throat
with their dreams and hopes,
it smokes, this place,
it burns, its chest,
is filled with phlegm,
it lets them go, infect
their homes.
Today, a warrior poet passes,
and the people will mourn
in transit,
the city will breathe in silence,
a quiet choir of violence
leaving their prayers behind them.

But, if you must go,
pack light,
your soul, it glows
and k(no)w,
this city has not turned you
to coal,
yet.

PHILLIPPA YAA DE VILLIERS

is a South African poet who teaches creative writing at Wits University, Johannesburg. She has published three collections and edited two anthologies. Her work appears in several local and international journals, including *Poetry Archive*, *Lyrikline* and *Badilisha*. She is a member of the editorial board of African Poetry Book Fund.

FOOTPRINT

I have fallen into myself, a ball pool of velvet and razor
spheres.
Asymptomatic, I flail and fumble and rest in the vaulted
darkness. Only now I notice the brilliance of stars
and the way their distance telescopes constantly
as a hand touches my chest. We've become one,
brightened by the dark shadow that shows us who we are.

Frankly I'd prefer to be outside transacting with the others,
maybe even looting a bottle store. On the surface.
But I'm trapped down here, spinning my solitude
into a web. Not coughing but catching flies, feeding on their
rude
energy of life.   Ignoring distress.   Sucked dry.

At times I feel terror I'll never return. What day is it?
My matter
as consequent as a snail's footprint on the pepper tree's trunk,
a long and silent tear, dried mucous on the patient bark.
And somewhere far from here or maybe near
someone is coughing into their last handkerchief,
attended by a pair of latex hands, a masked heart. Duty
spun into kindness.

I tune into news/disease for there but for the grace of god go I
my mother taught, although an atheist till the end, when
death vacuumed her up, like the dust she hated. She seemed
surprised. I see her still smiling in her own bed, spangled
with stars. It was a relief to stop the suffering. She refused
a funeral because she couldn't see the point.
'I won't be there.' Ironically in retrospective solidarity with
Iran,

Where The Virus buries people en masse, their name engraved
nowhere but on their own rememberer, who
ploughs their footsteps into the tomorrow land leaving
a frail   silver   t
                                  r
                                    a
                                      i
                                        l.

MEIFU WANG

is a poet and translator, born in Taiwan and now settled in the US. She is the editor and co-translator of *21st Century Chinese Poetry* (www.modernchinesepoetry.com). Her poetry has appeared in various literary journals in China, in Seattle-area local newspapers, and in *Denver Quarterly*.

ISOLATION OF THE ELDERLY

After you learn to steer a boat—
tacking upstream, backing into a cove,
down a narrow canal through a set of locks—
where will you go?
Son, will you not go?

I see the world from upstairs;
a lot is happening below us.
I watch my visitors getting dressed fabulously,
ready to leave for an evening concert
somewhere downstairs.

I don't know what to say: joyous for the young,
a little downcast for a communal life lost.
Then I see my boy gleaming with joy
emerging from a narrow canal,
ready to sail the open sea.

When I look up from the roof garden,
the sky is still blue,
riddled with puffy white clouds,
but this old country is now
another world.

EACH ONE A TRIBE

Call up my old shadows.
Have them come together as a tribe—
sunset on our backs,
heads at uneven heights,
we approach our village in the sizzling heat.

Who is the wise one?
Who have stumbled and cried?
Is there a sage among us?
Are we ready to face the next hardship?
When will the fair weather return?

Where do we go
to gather food for the winter?
Is today's me trustworthy to lead our tribe into tomorrow?
How do I choose the right track
away from danger?

Ah, here you are.
Now you are with me—
together a new tribe,
so many more heads!
Let us talk, let us work together.

You will be my eyesight,
I will be your rock.

LES WICKS

has been active in the Australian literary community for forty-five years. His fourteenth book of poetry, *Belief* (Flying Islands), was published in 2019. His work has been published in over 350 newspapers, anthologies and magazines across thirty countries and in fifteen languages. He is also a publisher and editor.

OUTDOOR EXERCISE ALLOWED

Last week
my bicycle complained
but eventually took me to Cronulla Beach.
It's a wealthy suburb Covid hotspot,
this disease took a liking to moneyed travellers.
Flawless lawn, blonde hair, bad politics
even the sun's muscles tone.
This area carries on just fine,
if only one could put make-up on a facemask.

The Merida Crosslands hybrid
has to be stored outside, a rough life.
This thing, like they say about dogs,
has taken on its owner's appearance.
Loose screws and rust, a pitted grey—
it still writes notes at the sky.

I ride daily
cantankerous memories crowd the bike-lane.
Then I stay inside
but talk more than ever. Is it worth more than touch?

Carolyn has fled her mind.
Across Europe they ask what is left.
From China my friend instagrams her first outside steps . . .
she's dressed up like it's a date with the universe.
There's no word from another friend in the Philippines
and Americans can't stop apologizing for their mess.
Everyone eats more
except those who can't—
I won't steal those stories.

My bike hums through emptier streets,
our weather has been polished up even
as they shut the borders.
Being Australia, of course they allow us the ocean,
social distance easy in the Pacific.
Alcohol sales hit new records

and I ride
past gardens, graves and supermarket queues.
On the intersection of Mimi St the machine is immobilized
by a flowering eucalypt. We wave to each other.
Families bond or disintegrate
and sometimes can't tell the difference.
By Forest Rd there are less cars
but they still howl like wolves.
It's a kind of ritual, everyone
understands and ignores it . . .
less dire than other assaults, they say
everyone has eluded mortality today.

Global warmhearted, people have marked everything
So with nothing left, retreat again to my reservation
(1970s' working-class apartment)
and there await developments.

Swap meals with my friend in #8
(Mustafa's a bit over-reliant on the meat—
me on the dairy—
we both believe in garlic and mushrooms)

Tomorrow I'll ride my bike by the bay,
my irrelevance is a sanctity.

DROUGHT TO BLAZE TO VIRUS

First there was no rain for months.
Fruit bats fell dead from the eucalypts
    magpies hurled out their barren nests.
Can't get any worse
but then cinders became our new black.
Carbonized leaves were the last filigree. Fire.

Towns burned.
The air was overcoat grey,
sometimes when bushfires were nearer,
                    shit-smeared apricot.
These were the last colours left.

A spitting spray hit soil, there was no permeation . . .
runoff scribbled obituary all down towards the town drains.
Even fire lost interest as it rooted about
the debris it mistook for forest floor.
Feathers hide in soot. Fur sits in dismal clumps
and this is no seasonal moult.

Saw Steve in November
    to know titans tire.
Fighting wildfires, he spent months out of town
to a point where the land wore his sweat
and he carried the smoke home to his partner.
Peter said he loves the solitude
but missed his man's hands
when he was away or just back, exhausted.

Woodchips are fashionable this year,
concrete paths don't burn
but occasionally I find something . . .

To be over . . .
which in turn is thrown again
Now the world sickens. Peter is immune-compromised
their community locked down.
Steve has been laid off.
They sit on the balcony
      watch the rain
            worry about everyone else.

ATHOL WILLIAMS

is a South African social philosopher and award-winning author of fourteen books. He is an acclaimed poet with over 100 poems published in literary journals and four published books of poetry. He has published seven children's books in the Oaky series. His autobiography is titled *Pushing Boulders: Oppressed to Inspired*. Athol serves on the board of the *South African Literary Journal* and is the founder of the Cape Flats Book Festival.

A DAY IN MARCH

The pigeons go hungry in Trafalgar Square;
they've not heard the news—there'll be no

half-eaten slice waiting near the fountain, or
hot chip dropped on the step; there'll be no

flake of pastry near Nelson's base, or
sesame seed at a lion's paw. Not today, not

for weeks, as scraps and crumbs are locked down, or
locked up, or locked away in love, with life.

INTO THE UNKNOWN

the earth knows only to spin, does it not?
and the river knows only to flow
and the wind to blow, like life
that knows only to keep living—the slave girl,
the rich heir, flooded with the desire to live;
the spritely calf, the weathered bull, they too
know only to keep breathing, to keep their hearts
clocking, like the silent lamb and crowing cock
who have all their cogs fitted to keep going,
to keep breath blowing, and blood flowing,
and the earth spinning, for this is all life knows.

BETWEEN SUMMERS

The vine does not die between summers, it does not lie
in the ground waiting for life to restart. Even in winter
the vine is awake to its heartbeat, every moment a gift.

In winter it clears out its shelves of leaves that've dried
and fortifies the beams that hold up its branches,
it strengthens the pumps that draw juice from the soil
and reboots its machines that turn sunlight to fruit.

Like summer, in winter, the vine continues to live;
no matter the season, it is living, not waiting for life.

ANNIE ZAIDI

is the author of *Prelude to a Riot, Gulab, Love Stories # 1 to 14*, and *Known Turf: Bantering with Bandits and Other True Tales*, and the co-author of *The Good Indian Girl*. She is the editor of *Unbound: 2000 Years of Indian Women's Writing*. She was awarded the Nine Dots Prize in 2019 for innovative thinking and the Hindu Playwright Award in 2018 for her play, *Untitled 1*. Her work has appeared in various anthologies and literary journals, including *The Griffith Review, The Aleph Review, The Charles River Journal, The Missing Slate* and *Out of Print*.

BEACH MEMORY

After she had cupped handfuls of municipal water over her
sandy toes
Put on the sandals he had knotted to his backpack
And watched him run her comb through his greasy hair as she sat
His motorcycle helmet in her lap, he took out the blue
Brown checked handkerchief from the pocket of his jeans and
folded it to the size of
Sponge wad in her compact which he knew was three shades
lighter than her skin
He held her chin with two fingers and a thumb
Wiped her nose
Forehead
Temples
Philtrum
Jaw
He shook the handkerchief loose and wiped his own face
Looked at his phone, said
Huh! As if I am going to go
Anywhere now.

APOCALYPSE

Waves do not come dashing against the noontide
They tiptoe in
and out with the smallest dose of pain
taken from the cabinet you left dusty
on purpose
so nobody guesses how much you hoard

The wretched manage to show up
across the shatterproof glass of time
to class office factory godown
boat ocean horizon end time
with a slouch and a glower
of expectation

Your eyes are fleet
testing
weighing
catlike
on nights when the tide rises
and rises and the rain quietly falls,
as promised, it comes

It sits
gleaming on the roof
with creature eyes
offering no sign
no pause for breath
no cause or rules
about arks: no ones or twos
it offers no map

A thing
squealing its lack of defence
mouse like, it comes to nibble
the cheese of your world

It arches
head and back
now signals: here
I am
Take me at this flood
or there I go.

ZINGONIA ZINGONE

is a poet, novelist and translator who writes in Spanish, Italian, French and English. Her poetry books have been published in Spain, Mexico, Colombia, Nicaragua, Costa Rica, Italy, France and India. A volume of her collected poems, *Songs of the Shulammite* (Colección Anverso, Uniediciones), was published in Colombia in 2019. She is editorial advisor of the Mexican literary magazine *El Golem*.

INTO THE NIGHT

In night's walk crossing
Voids
Lit up by crashing glasses
Taverns
Filled to rim with babble
Thoughts
Budding evergreen
Branching visions
Into primeval shades of darkness
Reality
Slowly sipped by idleness.

APOCALYPSE NOW

Christmas approaches.

Despite acid rain
Putrefied in pools
Among Roman cobblestones,
Mothers forced to kill their offspring
To survive,
Fireworks in Mumbai
Alas! No one
Buys chestnuts anymore.

Despite the great empty pocket.

Santa Claus on Piazza Navona
Raffles candies and delivers stones
—'tis a joke—
Children laugh.

Manolo begs for coins
Or is it Antonio or Giovanni
Pigeon poop's in the tin.

The list is long and governments
Stretch the quilt
Trying to cover all feet.

The sneezing index grows.
Vaccines are futile
And not enough for everyone.

A vicar fights poverty
Displaying a statue of the Virgin
Giving away second-hand clothes.

Yes, he won the elections.

Chinese sell toys
Toxic but affordable.

And yes, Christmas again
In heat and thunder,
Is Noah's Ark in your manger?

COPYRIGHT ACKNOWLEDGEMENTS

Amanda Bell, 'Buttercups' and 'Bumblebees', originally published in *First the Feathers* (Doire Press, 2017)

Maaz Bin Bilal, 'Who Did It', first published in *EPW*, Vol. 55, Issue No. 14, 4 April 2020

Mustansir Dalvi, 'My Room', first published in print in *To Catch a Poem: An Anthology of Poetry for Young People*, edited by Jane Bhandari and Anju Makhija, Sahitya Akademi, 2014; 'Kintsukuroi' was first published in *Cosmopolitician*, Poetrywala, 2018

Joy Harjo, 'I Give You Back', from *She Had Some Horses*, 1983, used by permission of W.W. Norton & Co., Inc

Ravi Shankar, 'Latin for Life', first published in 'The in / completeness of human experience', *Text* Special Issue, Number 58, 2020, *Text: Journal of writing and writing courses*, 24, 1 (April): 1-159. Available at http://www.textjournal.com.au/speciss/Issue58.pdf